CW00500314

Not All Coppers Are . . . . !

Not All Coppers Are . . . . !

A Gwent Policeman's Story

by

Paul Heaton

P.M. Heaton Publishing
Abergavenny, Gwent
Great Britain
1994

This book is dedicated to all those who have suffered in the name of Justice

ISBN 1 872006 03 5
© First Edition November, 1994: P.M. Heaton

Published by P.M. Heaton Publishing, Abergavenny, Gwent, NP7 9UH.
Printed by The Amadeus Press Ltd., Huddersfield, West Yorkshire, HD2 1YJ
Typesetting by Highlight Type Bureau Ltd., Shipley, West Yorkshire, BD17 7EG.

Author

Paul Michael Heaton was born at New Inn, Pontypool, in 1944 and was educated at Greenlawn Junior School in New Inn and the Wern Secondary School at Sebastopol. At fifteen he left school and commenced employment, at first in a local store and then with a builders' merchant. A year later he was appointed as a Deck Cadet in the Merchant Navy, with the Lamport and Holt Line of Liverpool, usually serving in the Brazil and River Plate trades. He joined the Monmouthshire Constabulary (now Gwent) in 1963 and served at Abergavenny, Cwmbran, Newport, the Traffic Department, as the Force Public Relations Officer, and for five years was the Wales Region Inspectors' Representative on the Joint Central Committee of the Police Federation of England and Wales.

He retired from the Police Service at the end of 1993, and has recently established his own publishing business. He is the author of sixteen books on Merchant Shipping and the Spanish Civil War. His other interests are breeding thoroughbred race horses and he has a growing flock of sheep.

Acknowledgements

I would like to thank all those who have had any part in assisting me in the compilation of this book, and particularly those photographic sources credited hereafter: Ernest Carver and Son Ltd., South Wales Argus, Robert Hitchings, Brian Knight, Western Mail, South Wales Echo, Gwent Constabulary, GREN, South Wales Constabulary, Daily Mail, Gwent Constabulary Joint Branch Board, the Joint Central Committee of the Police Federation of England and Wales, Lewis Productions Ltd. and John Pennington. I am also grateful to Glyn Harris for his pen and ink sketch which appears on the dust jacket.

Contents

Introduction

I served in the Police Service for thirty years. In that time there was much joy, and a little pain. Of my service, almost half was spent as a Motor Cyclist, and if I'm remembered for anything it will be that. This book is no crusade or exposé. It is my account, yes through my own eyes, so it will be my version and no others, of the things that happened to me. It is an invitation to laugh at and with me – because as I wrote the book I had to stop on more than one occasion to wipe the tears of laughter from my face. I had not realised that so many humorous things had happened to me, and that I could have survived having pulled so many little stunts. I salute all I worked with and particularly Bryan Giles Knight who was the best motor cyclist Gwent ever had – I know because I always considered myself to be only a strip of tyre rubber behind him.

The book deals with all aspects of my career, from a constable on the beat right through to Inspector in Force and at National level on the Federation. I had intended to give graphic accounts of the fatal road accidents I dealt with, but resisted, as it would have meant raking up old memories for people who have managed to or are still trying to re-establish their lives without a loved one. My thoughts are still with these brave people, and I wish them well for the future.

To Mr. Martin, Mr. Bevan, and Mr. Woods, who all had such a great influence on my life, I would hope that if they could read these words, that they would approve. They were my peers. Surprisingly, one often hears a Police Officer bemoaning the fact that all the characters have gone – not realising that they themselves are the characters of this new generation. Yes, what they do will be held up as the memories for those who follow.

The Police Service has been good to me – it helped bring up my family. There were fifteen poorly paid years which happily were followed by better times. But even when the pay was bad, there were many good times. I served under three distinguished Chief Constables, and happily all will be able to read my story. In any chapter of life there will be one or two who will have let the side down, but as the title indicates, it was only a few, as 'Not all coppers are ....' Quite the contrary, the vast majority of officers are there to help and support the public in any way they can, and take pride in that fact.

In these days of changing Government policies – the Police Federation has done, and is still doing, its part to ensure that officer' interests are protected, and more importantly that the public receives the Police Service which it deserves.

I have set out to offend no man. Let us not take ourselves too seriously, as when we depart, there will be someone equally as able to take our place. I hope that you, the reader, get as much pleasure from reading this book as I have had in remembering and writing it.

Paul Heaton
November 1994

In the Beginning

I was brought up in the village of New Inn, near Pontypool in the old County of Monmouthshire. My first four years were spent living at Number 61, The Highway, on the side of the main road through the village, which was in fact the main Newport to Abergavenny trunk road. My home was in a terrace, a few doors down at one end was the local Police Station, at the other end of the terrace was the Co-op shop. At the side of the Police Station was the entrance to Clarewain, and on the opposite corner was Mr. Elmore's butchers shop.

My earliest memories were of incidents which occurred when I was around three years old. I remember carrying my wooden toy Wellington bomber down the stairs at No. 61 and actually taking off, landing at the bottom in a crumpled and very tearful heap. I recall to my eternal shame sinking my teeth into Yvonne Herbert's arm, a girl a little older than myself, and even more vividly the corrective action taken by my father. Another incident, took place following a brush with a playmate, Rhys Ashcroft. I don't actually recall the original battle, but remember as if it were yesterday, standing in front of Rhys' mother holding a stone which I was threatening to throw, and being chased home just in time to have a change of underwear.

Two other incidents stand out in my memory, both concerning our local Policeman – Stan Bevan. Mr. Bevan had a son a little younger than myself, and I often played with him. The problem was that his father had a stray dog and on the eventful day we let it out of the yard, and it promptly and tragically got run over by a car turning around in Clarewain. Mr. Bevan was not very happy with us, at all. My next brush with the Law, was when I led a group of my playmates down to the bank of the River Afon Lwyd, which wasn't too far from our homes. I, and some of my friends were really enjoying our paddle in the fast running coal-stained river when Mr. Bevan spoilt our fun, dragged us all out and led us home with more than a few chosen words. Again I vividly remember the subsequent ordeal by 'slipper' imposed by my father.

When I was almost five my parents decided to move, and we went to live in Lower New Inn, just around the corner from the public house of that name, in Lancaster Road at No. 2. My home for the next fourteen years was to be one of those marvellously fitted out post-war prefabs. There were in fact a hundred prefabs on the estate, but New Inn was a much sought after area in which to live, and we were surrounded by lovely neighbours. Down the lane from my home was a series of cottages, at the first of which a schoolfriend John Beames and his family lived, next door was the Jones' of which the two eldest boys Alan and Michael stand out in my memory. Much further down the lane lived Charlie Taylor, my childhood hero. Charlie was a very strong character, and if you were in his gang, you won at everything. We played soccer and cricket against other village boys from Clarewain, the New Houses and Ruth Road, and I can't remember ever being on the losing side. I was no sportsman, but it didn't matter, Charlie and a few others were so outstanding at whatever they did, that we just couldn't lose. Charlie was a winner, never a

A very young Paul Heaton when he had plenty of hair, with his big brother John.

loser, it wasn't in his vocabulary.

After a year or so in Lower New Inn, the local Bobby, Mr. Bevan, was promoted to Sergeant and moved on. However my parents kept in touch with him and his wife, and on one occasion Mrs. Bevan, a lovely lady, came to babysit whilst my parents went out to some function. I remember that my brother had a friend to stay, and he being five years older, was particularly irritating on this evening. I hadn't yet been put to bed, and when I couldn't stand my brother John any longer, not having any ammunition, I clouted him over the head with the butt of my toy rifle, laid him out proper, real blood flowing and everything. My parents were hurriedly called home from their evening out, and my father's slipper was much in evidence again, just as it had been at No. 61.

By this time a new village Bobby had been appointed, and he was the very stern faced, but in retrospect nonetheless kindly, Mr. Woods. Originally stationed in the Police Station near my former home, he subsequently moved to a new purpose-built building at Berry's Corner, next to the Traves' shop. He and his wife had three children, a son John who often played with the Lower New Inn boys, and two stunningly attractive daughters, Marylyn and Pat. We often played cricket on one of Mr. Jack Lewis' fields at the bottom of the lane below the Congregational Church, and sometimes Mr. Lewis' two younger sons, David and Brynley, were in our team. It didn't matter that the field was their father's because if we saw Mr. Woods coming we didn't wait around to find out if he wanted to talk to us, we automatically took off at top speed, such was our respect, or was it fear of him? He was not a man to whom you would ever show anything other than respect. That respect, had considerable effect on us. Very few of us got into any real kind of trouble. If you saw him walking down the street, you stopped breathing until he had passed by your door.

Enough of my childhood memories – but before we move on, I should mention the amazing fact that Lancaster Road, or more specifically Nos. 2 to 7, was to provide the Police Service with a considerable number of employees in the coming years. I lived at No. 2 and I joined the Monmouthshire constabulary when I was nineteen. At No. 3 lived the Atkins family, whose middle daughter became a typist in the Police Headquarters and subsequently worked in the Force Operations Room. She married a Policeman who joined a month after me, and he became a Sergeant. At No. 4 Phil Hale joined the Force, and his mother was caretaker at Pontypool Police Station. Joe Martin, who had served for thirty years, lived at No. 5 and when he retired became Sergeant Martin at Pilkington's Glass Works, in charge of security, where, incidentally, my father worked. Mr. Martin's son John joined the 'job' and was a Detective Superintendent when he retired. There was no Police connection at No. 6 that I know of, but the Green family at No. 7 provided a son for the Gwent Constabulary, and his sister married a man who rose to the rank of Inspector. Not a bad record for such a small area. Much must have been attributable to Sergeant Martin and Mr. Woods.

Years later, and even when I was promoted Sergeant, whenever I met Mr. Woods, who remained a constable throughout his service, I never called him Glyn, I always addressed him as Mr. Woods, I felt that to call him anything else would have been most disrespectful.

I Joined the Monmouthshire Constabulary

Having failed the 11-plus, I attended school at the Wern Secondary Modern at Sebastopol, until I was fifteen. Thereafter I worked for six months at the Woolworth's Store in Pontypool, followed by a similar period in the showroom at the builders merchants – the Clarence Trading Company at Pontymoile. Those were the days when you could finish one job on a Saturday and start another on Monday. Unemployment was not a word I had heard of.

Anyway, when I was sixteen I decided that I wanted to go to sea. I duly wrote off four letters to well known shipping companies and having replies from three, decided on an interview with the Lamport and Holt Line of Liverpool. I well remember going to see my former headmaster, Melville Jones at his home on a Sunday, and was rewarded with an excellent reference, which wasn't bad considering he believed in using the cane, and I had felt the end of it on more than one occasion. However in my reference he stated that I had obtained eleven subjects in the Certificate of Education (which was only the local examination). I attended with my father at the Liverpool office of the shipping company for an interview, where the Marine Superintendent commented that they had never had an application from anyone with eleven G.C.E.s before. My mouth opened to make an honest explanation, and a muffled yell came out, having been squarely kicked on the shin by my father. I got the message, and I got the job. I was Cadet Paul Heaton of the Merchant Navy. That is another story, but is interesting to point out that there are only 168 hours in a week, I know, because for the next three years I usually worked 112 of them.

Having almost reached the age of nineteen I decided that a life on the ocean wave was not for me. The pay even for a Cadet was good, and they paid overtime. The problem was you never stopped work, at sixteen I was around nine stone in weight, and almost three years later I was at least half a stone lighter. When I came home at the end of a voyage I slept for two days. No more bilge diving for me – but what was I going to do?

I had just spent three years in the Merchant Navy. I was nineteen all but, and I had worn a uniform, or I had when I was having my meals, I was in dungarees at all other times. I went and had a chat with Joe Martin, and he told me about the Police Service. This was interesting, as it came from a man that I was extremely fond of. Mr. Martin had given me a Player's cigarette when I was six and I went home and told my Dad that I didn't want pop and sweets anymore, I wanted beer and cigs. There was hell to play. Anyway having had my chat, I decided to apply to join the Monmouthshire Constabulary. I didn't write off to the Headquarters in Abergavenny, I just turned up and was furnished with an application form, there being plenty of vacancies. My height was measured, and I went home to fill in the form.

Duly completed I posted my application off. Various enquiries were made into my character, and Mr. Woods called. I was subsequently told to attend

Navigating Officer Cadet Paul Heaton in the Merchant Navy at 16 years of age.

at Pontypool Police Station, where the Sergeant told me to go to Boots the chemists to get weighed, and to bring the ticket back. He could see that I was woefully underweight, and being an obvious ex-Serviceman, gave me a parcel, which I was to hold when I was weighed. Even with the parcel I only just made 10 stone 4 pounds – God bless him.

I was one of about eight who attended at Abergavenny for an interview. The man in charge was Inspector Donald Wilding, who was assisted by Sergeant Don Rossiter and Constable Terry Fry. The tests completed, those of us still in the running went to the Doctor's surgery for an examination, followed by a chest X-ray at Nevill Hall Hospital. By this time there were four of us left, we were all appointed, and allocated our collar numbers – Constable 420 Hywel Lewis who had some previous service, Constable 421 Michael Charles Wyatt who had been a Police Cadet, Constable 422 Paul Michael Heaton, and Constable 423 Bernard Lewis. We would have to come back another day to be fitted out for uniform, we were told.

Having returned and filled three suitcases with uniform and equipment, it was arranged that I would have to attend at Pontypool Magistrates' Court to be sworn-in. Come the day, all smartly dressed in my uniform, Mr. Woods called to collect me and take me to the court. Wearing the uniform indoors was O.K., it was a different story once I stepped out of the house. I had an awful feeling of self consciousness. I was sworn in by the Chairman of the Bench, Councillor Mabel Lee, in the presence of Superintendent Jack Haines, both of whom said they knew my father Sam. Superintendent Haines suggested that I might like to stay and see some of the Court proceedings – how could I refuse? Thereafter I spent around three hours listening to a variety of cases, but didn't absorb any useful knowledge.

When the Magistrates adjourned for lunch, it was time for me to set course for home. Unfortunately Mr. Woods, who was a busy man, had left, and I had to walk the couple of hundred yards from the Court building to the bus stop – it seemed as if I walked for miles. I was dressed in uniform, what if someone should ask me something. Here I was walking through the streets in full Police uniform, with a head which was empty of any kind of knowledge of the Service it represented. At last I reached the bus stop – but no bus – when would it come? I felt very uncomfortable – I felt more like a pantomime horse than a Policeman, and were people looking at me. At last the bus came – I let everyone get on before me, then I climbed the steps and sat down about half way down the bus. We still had conductors then. I offered my fare, but he wouldn't accept it. What if a Bus Inspector should get on. The bus travelled from the Town Hall at Pontypool, stopped at the Clarence, again at Rockhill Road, up Usk Road, and stopped at the Turnpike. Hell, it had to happen to me – a bus inspector got on. Will he ask me for my ticket? I'll get the sack on my first day. He walked up the bus inspecting passengers' tickets. As he got closer to me I must have been beetroot red, but thankfully he passed and didn't ask me to produce a ticket. Finally the bus got to the end of my road, and I walked quietly, but hurriedly to my door. Thank God I've made it home.

The most difficult thing about becoming a Police Officer is getting used to wearing the uniform.

Basic Training

When I had been interviewed a month or so earlier by the Assistant Chief Constable, Bill Farley, he had indicated that my Merchant Navy background should hold me in good stead for the future. I had already been part of a disciplined body. The post-war Police Service was manned by ex-servicemen, men who had fought for their country, men who had endured hardships, men who knew what life was all about. Then followed a generation who had undergone National Service, and whilst they had not suffered the privations of their peers, they nonetheless knew what life was all about, and had belonged to a group who in the main had that magic ingredient as far as the Police Service was concerned, 'common sense'.

Now, here was I, from a generation who had not known service life, had not worn a uniform, and had not served their country. We were the children of the 'forties'. We were the children of parents who had seen to it that we enjoyed the privileges that they had not known. A result of our parents' endeavours, was that we had to an extent been spoilt. We had it made. The 1960s was the period of full employment. If you didn't have a job, it was because you didn't want one. Pay in the Police was relatively poor, and as a result there were thousands of vacancies throughout the country. Our lack of worldly experience meant that we were the first generation in the history of the service who had not learnt common sense, and many of our number, never having been away from home, were naive to say the very least.

It was against this background that, on December 30, 1963 I reported to the No. 8 District Police Training Centre at Bridgend. I was met by Sergeant Norman Thomas of the Glamorgan Constabulary, who was seconded to the Training Centre, and was for the next thirteen weeks to be our Class Instructor. One other had arrived before me, that was Brian Thomas of Pembrokeshire, who had seen some service in Scotland with the British Transport Police. I heard our Norman say to him that he was well suited to become the Class Leader for the course. If only I had arrived ten minutes earlier.

Our class consisted of nineteen men, ten of whom, including myself were housed in a dormitory in the main building, whilst the other nine were to spend the next thirteen weeks sleeping in a tatty looking wooden hut around the back. We embarked on the first stage in our Police career, some with trepidation, some with apprehension as to what the next thirteen weeks were to have in store. I was surprised by the number who were so obviously homesick. It was clear that some of our number were away from home for the first time. Our Norman explained that this was to be no easy course, and that we would have to put in extra time to ensure that we got the results which would ensure our continued existence in the Police. I was vaguely amused, as I found the 44 hour week very much to my liking. Three square meals a day and a full nights sleep every night. You even had a day and a half off every week – who could ask for anything more?

I did say three square meals a day – that is correct, but it was the usual

**No. 8 District Police Training Centre, Bridgend. Basic Course.
December 30, 1963 - March 26, 1964.**

Back row (left): P.C.s A. Stubbs (Cardiff City), G. Bowen (Swansea), Colin Maddy (Herefordshire), Tony Parkhouse (Mid Wales), Mike Wyatt (Monmouthshire), H. Roberts (Gwynedd), Bob Ralphs (Herefordshire), J. Powell (Cardiff City).
Centre row: P.C.s D. Crees (Mid Wales), G. Beaudette (Glamorgan), W. Halstead (Denbighshire), Paul Heaton (Monmouthshire), Bernard Lewis (Monmouthshire), D. Guy (Swansea), F. Hill (Glamorgan), B. George (Swansea), R. Jones-Hughes (Denbighshire).
Front row: P.C. Brian Thomas (Pembrokeshire), Sgt. C. Edwards (Instructor), Sgt. Norman Thomas (Instructor), Inspector Tom O'Connell (Instructor), Superintendent J. Graves (Deputy Commandant), Sgt. Goff Arnold (Instructor), Sgt. J. Anderson (Instructor), P.C. Dick Ashman (Swansea).

(Ernest Carver & Son Ltd.)

results of canteen cooking. The food was I'm sure excellent before the cook got hold of it, but alas by the time that it appeared on the plate it was runny, burnt, dry, or in some other way had its edible qualities removed. It was stodge, plain and simple. No problem, the Training Centre had its own shop where you could fill up on other more palatable things – I wonder if the cook had shares in the shop?

On the first morning we were all introduced to Goff Arnold, the legendary Drill Instructor. This man was to have the undoubted pleasure of converting the nineteen of us into a smart disciplined body of men, who could march and look the part. However, on this first morning no one would have envied him his task. As we all know, when you march your left arm goes out in tandem with your right leg, and your right arm with your left leg, or so they should. It took Goff Arnold the full thirteen weeks to achieve this, and even then one of our number was still trying to put left arm with left leg, and right with right. It was as well that Sergeant Arnold was able to burn off his frustrations in some other way. Months later, having finished our course, he featured in the National Press – even the Sunday papers covered the story, of how a new recruit had left the centre after only a few days – citing Goff Arnold's vocabulary as one of the main reasons. I had spent three years at sea, and he still came out with swear words that were new to me. Whilst he made a loud noise, well a hell of a din, he was in fact quite a kindly soul, and took obvious pride in what he had achieved by the time of our passing out parade.

Sport was heavy on the agenda. I qualified to Bronze Medallion at life saving. We played rugby, a sport that I had never excelled at. It was one of those unfortunate turns of events when I received a kick to my unmentionables, and had to report to the Matron. She being quite elderly knew exactly what to do, she said "Have a cold bath twice a day – the swelling will soon go down". Well she was exactly right, and she didn't even look at the injured part, let alone touch it.

At school, the only sport that I nearly excelled at was cross country running. It was good that the centre had it on the list of activities. I had learnt, that in cross country, if you wanted to be at or near the front at the finish, you had to start off at the front. There was no way you could make up ground half way around the course. Anyway, a coach dropped us off about ten miles away at a pub called the Pelican, hence the event was called the Pelican run, and we finished back at the Training Centre. Mike Wyatt from Monmouthshire was particularly good at cross country, and three of us used to stay together in the lead, he would finish first, and I in third place, or this was what happened on the first two runs. On the third he and his mate decided they were going to stride out and leave me within a mile or so of the finish, and that really is the story of how I came first, because the pair of them took the wrong turning further up the course. The centre was so impressed with our achievements in this field that they entered a team in a road race around the local Industrial Estate. It never pays to be good at anything. We used to finish at the Centre at lunchtime on Saturday and return on Sunday by 10pm. However, the race that we were press ganged into took place on a Saturday afternoon, so we wouldn't get home until the evening. Alas, the

Commandant's dreams were soon shattered. He couldn't have realised that the field was made up of some of the country's top runners. Well we did our best – we came in last, last but one, and last but two, and three didn't even complete the course. He didn't enter us again!

Like all groups, we did some stupid things. Whenever there was a new intake, at about one in the morning someone dressed up as a vicar, and another as a sergeant, and visited the newcomers dormitory where their naiveté showed. They were persuaded to get out of bed and say prayers, and I was always amazed that no one in authority visited to see why there was hymn singing going on in the early hours.

I finished the course, being placed thirteen out of nineteen, and both Mike Wyatt and Bernard Lewis from Monmouthshire did better than that. So, effectively, I was last out of the Monmouthshire contingent. Never mind. Of the sixteen students who were from other forces, it surprises me that I have only met two in the last thirty years. They are Dick Ashman from Swansea who I last saw at the South Wales Police Driving School at Bridgend where he was an instructor, and Colin Maddy from Herefordshire who was working for a tobacco company, having left the force a few years later. It was as well that I was a smoker. I did hear of one of our number who was unfortunate enough to have a run in with a crowd of yobs, and was left handcuffed to some railings until rescued by firemen. I'm not mocking, it could have happened to me.

Her Majesty's Inspector of Constabulary Neil Galbraith, CBE.
Formerly Chief Constable of Monmouthshire.
(South Wales Argus)

15

On the Beat

Easter Bank Holiday Tuesday is one of the busiest days of the year in Abergavenny. Not only is it market day, with an open market, but there is also the normal cattle market on a day when everyone converges on the town from the neighbouring areas to enjoy themselves and have what has become a family day out. Traffic queues back for miles, and it takes ages to reach the town centre, where the nightmare of parking was still to face you.

It was on such a day as this that I was to report to Police Headquarters in the town for the customary interview with the Chief Constable following initial training. The Headquarters building was a fine old structure at the junction of the Hereford Road with Lower Monk Street, which at that time was the main road from South Wales to the North. Having managed to park my car, a grey Austin Cambridge borrowed from my father, I made my way to the building. On arrival I was shown into the Chief Constable's office, where I met, for the first time, the head of the Monmouthshire Constabulary – Neil Galbraith, a distinguished looking Scot. After a short interview, standing up in front of my seated leader, I was told to report to Abergavenny Police Station, to which station I was being posted for duty.

I walked through the town towards the Police Station which was situated in Baker Street. I no longer felt so self conscious in my uniform, but nonetheless I tingled with excitement as anyone does who is about to embark on a new chapter in life. Here I am – its the real thing – a Bobby at last. A real one.

On arrival I was shown into the Inspector's office where I met the Sub-Divisional Commander, Inspector Wilf Evans, who wanted to know all about me. He had been a Welsh Rugby International decades earlier, and this belied the fact that he was a quiet, kindly man, who cared about people in general, and for those who served under him most particularly. I was lucky, very very lucky. I had drawn the long straw, because here was a man who led by example. A man who was not taken to ranting and raving, but a man who was blessed with the qualities of leadership, which enabled him to extract the best from all who served under him. He was a man everyone admired, and would be ashamed to let him down. My interview with him completed, he showed me around the Police Station, introducing me to all who were on duty. I can't remember how many constables were stationed at Abergavenny, but there were two sergeants – Frank Williams, who was a native of Sebastopol where I had gone to school, and who was in a few months to transfer to the Traffic Department, and Jack Godfrey who in later years was to spend so much of his service on C.I.D. The building was old, with offices, cells, an enquiry office, and a small kitchen on the ground floor, and the Magistrates' Court upstairs. Next door, but really an interim part of the building was the Inspector's house, where he lived with his wife and two children.

Those were the days when one worked eleven days out of fourteen, with three days off. A 44 hour working week, with no paid overtime of any kind and, as I recall, two weeks leave annually. The duty roster reflected the needs of the town, but generally worked out that each officer had two weeks of nights, one week of evenings, one week of afternoons, one of early mornings with one of 9 to 5 days. That's how it was supposed to work, but with holidays, sickness and training requirements, this pattern was subject to change.

They were also the days when single men had to live in the town in which they were stationed, and I was duly fixed up with lodgings in a house in Park Avenue – with a kindly spinster. My bedroom was adequately large, with a double bed, but there were three comfortable chairs in the room, and to reach my pillow I had to climb over at least two. Some months later I moved digs to Albert Road, with a married couple, next door to Robert Jones who lived at home with his mother, and was stationed with me.

My first proper shift was on nights. I arrived at the Police Station at 9.30pm, was briefed by the Sergeant at 9.45pm and set out with the other night man, Roger Tuck, at 10pm to check the lock-ups. We proceeded down through the town from the Monument, through Frogmore Street, High Street and Cross Street, to the Bus Station, where we checked the Bus Depot, and that all was well. If we found a door accidentally left unlocked we contacted the keyholder to put matters right. If premises had been broken into, a search ensued, and action was taken to secure it. Yes, there were only two night men, one on evenings (6pm – 2am), and a sergeant or senior outstation man to supervise, but only for the earlier part of the night. At 2am the two night men were on their own, one in and one out. Why should Abergavenny tremble.

When I had been at sea I had read in the English language newspaper – The Buenos Aires Herald of the Queen's visit to Abergavenny a year or two earlier. The report had stated that the people of Abergavenny were so poor that they couldn't afford a red carpet for the town hall steps, and had in fact painted them red. Sure enough, when I was ejecting combatants from one of the Saturday night dances I often used to bounce down the steps, and they were red. In fact when some of my precious blood was spilt it didn't show at all.

One thing stood out from my training at Bridgend, whenever there was a fight in progress, walk don't run. If you ran to the fight, you became part of it and risked injury. Far better to walk, let those who wanted to use their energy up, turn up quietly and arrest them in a much more orderly fashion. On one such occasion I was with Mansel Thompson, and some time earlier a group of local tow-rags had beaten a Brynmawr boy up. The valley boys had cornered the local culprits in Market Street, and by the time we had reached the scene 'Justice' had been done, and the local ring leader was wearing the marks of their revenge.

One night I was working with Des Rogers when we got a message from the Police at Monmouth to the effect that a Ford Consul which had been stolen from Worcester sometime earlier was enroute towards us with three youths aboard. Having just taken delivery of a Commer Cob van Des drove out along the Monmouth Road to meet the vehicle. This was exciting stuff, I'd never had anything like this to deal with before. Sure enough the offending vehicle came into sight, we turned and followed it, and eventually stopped it by the traffic lights at the junction of High Street with Frogmore Street. There were three of them, and two of us. We realised that if a run ensued we could only hope to catch two, they realised it as well. We decided

Monmouthshire Constabulary – Monmouth Division July, 1964.

Back row (left): P.C.s Glyn Roberts, Granville Fox, Ron Day, John Price, Bert Wilkins, Bill Hughes, Cedric Eynon, Dick Stevens, Reg Childs. *Third row*: P.C.s Paul Heaton, John Whitcombe, Pete Worthing, unidentified, D.C.s Bryn West, Jim Adams, D. Sgt. Bill Williams, D.C.s Fred Diggins, Ray Eustace. P.C.s Bryan Williams, Ken Gardner, Merv Vaughan, Colin Gay. *Second row*: P.C.s Dennis Bayliss, Bob Jones, Tony Coleman, Brian Nelmes, unidentified, Les Tyler, Dai Lloyd, John Jenkins, Lou Barrett, John Hewes, Bernard Mitchell, Wyndham Lewis, Les Price, Charlie Irwin, Olly Catley. *Front row*: P.C. Lou Edmunds, Sgts. Bryn Pugh, John Godfrey, Bill Harris, George Green, Insp. Charlie Hinley (Chepstow Sub-Divisional Commander), Insp. Frank Davies (Monmouth Sub-Divisional Commander), Superintendent Ronald Scott (Divisional Commander), Insp. Wilf Evans (Abergavenny Sub-Divisional Commander), P. W. Anne Le Trail, Sgts. Jack Pritchard, Fred Jones, Len Barber, Harry Drake, Edgar Shepherd.

18

to leave the vehicles blocking the road, and to walk them up Lewis' Lane straight to the front door of the Police Station. By luck, judgement, call it what you want, we managed to get all three in the station. Des searched each one, and we then locked them in a single cell. On the Charge Sheet, they had refused to give their names and addresses, I had written Green, Red and Blue, to identify each, as they had three coloured sweaters on. I learnt an important lesson that night, as the cheeky little beggars all swopped sweaters. Never mind, it wasn't long before the Worcester Police sent an escort to remove them back to their area.

It was once unkindly said, when it was known that I was going to be stationed at Abergavenny, "Abergavenny is full of Pubs, Dogs and Prams". There certainly were a lot of pubs. I had in fact seen a number of prams. And my word there were a lot of dogs. Stray dogs were put in a kennel at the back of the station, and they weren't always very quiet. Inspector Evans' sleep was often disturbed, and on such occasions it was the instruction for the officer who had to check the commercial premises on the outskirts of the town to take the dog with him for a walk, and thereby giving Baker Street at least a couple of hours peace and quiet. Thirty years or so on, and with a changing town, I cannot exactly recall my route, but I do remember it was a very lonely couple of hours. There were no personal radios then – if you had a problem you shouted for help, and hopefully someone would open a window and ask what the problem was. If you were lucky you would reach a phone box. Returning to the dogs, I actually found it a comfort to have a dog with me when I took this lonely road. It helped give me courage.

There had been a series of break-ins in an office in the town. When I got to work it was announced that two officers were to be locked in this office for the night to try and catch the culprit. Whilst there was a telephone if help was needed there was no water. My landlady always gave me a small bottle of milk, just enough for two cups of tea, and that's all the fluid I had to drink all night. My colleague, however, had two big flagons of lemonade, and it's difficult to relate but the mean devil drank the whole lot in front of me, saying "That's your problem". There is justice in the world – many years later I heard the story of how this officer had entered the passageway of the King's Head Hotel in Cross Street, at the moment someone turned the lights out. When the lights came back on 'this officer' was found laid out on the floor. Bless you Albert.

Nothing happened in the office that night, and for the following two nights I kept observation there alone, but suitably provisioned. On the morning of my last night shift I was let out at 5am went back to the station for a cup of tea, and at 5.30am just as the first signs of dawn were appearing, I went back to check the premises. As I approached I looked up and saw what appeared to be someone on the roof. Not having any means of communication, and fearing that the culprit would escape, I was reluctant to leave the scene. I therefore stopped a lorry that was going north, and asked the driver if he would summon assistance for me. He departed, and I continued my vigil. It was getting lighter now, and I noticed that as I moved on the pavement the culprit also moved high overhead on the roof. It was then that I realised my mistake. Hell, what I thought I had seen was actually the chimney of the roof of the building adjacent to the office. As I moved I had seen it at a different angle, thinking that it was the figure of a person. How on earth was I going to explain this. Just as I had discovered my error, the troops began to arrive. A Traffic Patrol car with Mike Dixon and another aboard, George Verrier who had left the Force Operations Room unmanned in order to help an officer he feared was in trouble, Reg Childs the dog handler together with his dog fresh from their respective beds, the other night man on duty in Abergavenny – having locked the station, together with a still bleary-eyed Inspector Evans who although only just called from his slumbers was immaculately turned out, as only he could. Alas there was nowhere for me to hide. I explained my honest mistake to the Inspector and he could see my acute embarrassment. He made me feel much better, stating that "if there had been someone there, we would have surely caught him", and it was the best kind of mistake to make. To everyone's credit not one person laughed, as I may have done myself. I should mention I was never used on observations ever again during my period on the beat.

There was a considerable amount of commercial traffic travelling through the town, and I well remember the course that two A.E.C. articulated lorries took on their journey north. Both had set out from the Usk Road Depot of the British Road Services with glass carried in a type of metal pallet. The first lorry driven by Jack Rutter of Abergavenny reached Pontrilas when his load slipped from the bed of the trailer, all across the ground. The lorry behind, driven by John Young, only reached the Hardwick roundabout at the entrance to the town before its load fell from the vehicle all over the road. I had nothing to do with the Pontrilas incident as it was outside our area, in Herefordshire. But the 14 tons of glass which were spread over the road at Hardwick needed a fleet of tipper lorries and a mechanical shovel to clear. Mr. Young was never prosecuted for this. The previous Saturday night a Police Officer had been in considerable difficulty with a group of youths outside a dance held in St. Hilda's Church Hall in Griffithstown. Badly assaulted, the first person to come to his aid was John Young who saved him from further injury, and assisted with the arrests. So it was that the lorry driver received an 'official caution' for the insecure load, however, his colleague was less fortunate. It is interesting, but my Father worked for Pilkingtons the Glass Works at Pontypool, and he told me that as a result of these incidents new trailers with improved suspension had to be designed.

One day I was rostered to work 2pm – 10pm (afternoons), and dutifully turned up at 1.30pm, whereupon I was told by the sergeant to go home, I wasn't supposed to be in work until 4pm. I couldn't understand this, as the Duty Roster showed me down for a 2 – 10 shift, however he showed me the big board in his office with coloured flags denoting me as an unusual 4 – 12, but on further inspection in the duty register I was down for evenings (6pm – 2am). Well no matter what I was supposed to work, he, the sergeant, wanted me at 4pm, and 4pm he had me, right on the dot, breathing resentment, and in a right mood. As a result of this little incident I decided to try pastures new, and hearing of a vacancy on the Traffic Department as a Motor Cyclist I banged in an application there and then.

My last working day at Abergavenny on the beat was December 26, 1964 – Boxing Day, on a day shift. There had been a case of Anthrax, a deadly disease, in a horse, just outside the town. The means of disposal for a carcass in such cases is to dig a big pit and burn it before covering the hole over again. No I didn't dig the hole, but I spent most of my shift in the back of a railway wagon at the Brecon Road Railway yard filling the sacks full of coal which were to burn it.

Motor Cyclists at the Traffic Yard, Abergavenny in 1964.
P.C.s Bob Hitchings (Left), Mansel Thompson and John Moxham.

A Motor Cyclist Am I

I had never ridden a motor cycle. I had passed my driving test for cars about two months before joining the Police and my father owned a new Norton 600cc Big 4 combination for five years from 1952. My brother owned a couple in the past, a Matchless 250cc and a Norman Sport 250, but I had never felt the urge to tear around on two wheels. Yet here I was at 9am. on December 27, 1964 about to embark on a career as a Police Motor Cyclist. Alas, the weather was bad, too bad for motor cycling, and it was to be a week or two before my experiences on two wheels commenced.

Meanwhile Les Peard who started on Traffic the same day as a Patrol car driver was receiving some tuition, and I spent a few days out with him. He was actually under instruction from Len Reynolds, an experienced traffic man who was the driving instructor. When he had finished with Les, he would be teaching me. The one incident during these couple of days was when Len took us up over the top of Pontypool towards Abertillery. There was a fair bit of snow on the ground and this had built up in the centre of the track. We were in a heavy old Austin Westminster, and the car got stuck in the tracks, or more correctly the bottom of the car was stuck on the centre of a track with all four wheels off the road. A bit like a grounded whale. We couldn't get forward or backwards. It took a hell of a lot of work to get traction again, including the strategic placing of four coconut mats from the car under the wheels. I was pretty light before this escapade, but I swear I lost even more weight. By this time, however, I was a little over ten stone, but I could still play a tune on my ribs.

There were four other motor cyclists, Tony Eden, a mature hard-working sort who was in fact the senior man, Bob Hitchings from Pontypool, Mansel Thompson with whom I had previously worked at the local station, and Mike Wyatt with whom I joined. To go on the bikes was a route towards the motor patrol, and most who went via that route were really looking to get on the cars. The machines consisted of an A.J.S. 650 which was Tony Eden's, the index number was I think 792 CWO. Bob Hitchings, and Mansel had two not too old B.S.A. 650's, 517 and 518 JAX, Mike Wyatt had 214 EWO a B.S.A. 650cc Gold Flash, and if I made it I was to have the same type – 213 EWO. There were a number of smaller sized machines used on outstation duties, and another Gold Flash used as a Divisional bike at Abertillery – 215 EWO.

Whilst Len Reynolds was finishing off Les Peard's course, Tony Eden took me over from the Traffic Yard at the rear of the Police Headquarters to the Fairfield in Abergavenny, where he taught me the basics of motor cycling, and managed to get me to lift my feet off the ground. That must have taken him three hours, and I'm sure he never thought I would make a motor cyclist. Well if he didn't, neither did I. The very next morning, Len found me some old kit, a rather holey Barbour suit, and brought out a 250cc A.J.S. which was used for training. We were in business. He went ahead and I followed at a rather slow turn of speed. We rode up the Hereford Road from headquarters and turned right into Ross Road, thereafter having found third gear we crawled up the hill past Maindiff Court Hospital, and then turned right just before the Wernddu junction. By this time I was starting to settle down, and just as well because Len wasn't going to put up with me for long if I didn't get a move on. So by now I was travelling up hill and had found out how to open the throttle out. However, the next couple of hundred yards are a bit hazy in my memory. I know I started to negotiate a bend, and the next thing I was lying on the road with the bike on top of me. After a few seconds I heard loud laughter, and then my instructor was pulling the machine off me. I got up, slightly bruised, my pride completely in tatters, and then Len showed me the wet mud all across the road, obviously left by a farm tractor. When you drive a car, you don't fall off if you hit wet mud. It's different on a motor bike. It was a useful lesson to learn, and so early in the journey. I wasn't damaged, the bike wasn't damaged, so we plodded on, as Len said "You've got to get better".

By the next day I had reached all of sixty miles per hour. We were travelling from the direction of Chepstow towards Newport, down Pwllmeyric Hill and approaching the entrance to the St. Pierre Golf and Country Club, and fairly flying, when the engine seized up, and the bike came to a grinding halt. It was clear that the bike wasn't going anywhere. I was to leave it somewhere safe and wait for a Patrol car to pick me up to take me back to Abergavenny, whilst Len went off in search of another bike for me to wreck. Near where the bike had died was a bungalow, so I knocked on the door and asked the elderly lady who answered if I could leave it there until someone collected it. The bike had Police written all over the faring, but I'll always remember what she said. "Leave your name and address just in case the Police want to know whose it is". And I thought by now that I was beginning to look like a Policeman. Oh to see oneself as others see you. After about forty minutes Terry Jayne and Denis Parfitt turned up in their allocated car, a Westminster CAX 84B, on their way back from working the Chepstow Road and returned me to Abergavenny.

The very next day, actually Day 3, I continued my training, this time on a Francis Barnett 197cc. It wouldn't go fast enough for Len, so after two days, he persuaded Ken Pritchard to give me a test. Sergeant Pritchard was the Workshops Manager, but was one of two sergeants who gave driving tests, and were authorised to give DOT Pass Certificates. This time we went out on the Ross Road, but didn't turn right after Maindiff Court, and continued towards Skenfrith. We came back to Headquarters where I was given some sensible words of advice – "Try not to kill yourself" – and I was qualified, and it only took four days. However, Len wasn't completely happy, and he took me out the following day, my last under instruction. I was riding my beloved and decrepid B.S.A. Gold Flash, index number: 213 EWO.

A day or two later I had to accompany whoever was on patrol, whilst they showed me the area and showed me the ropes. I assisted with a couple of wide loads, which we escorted from Glangrwney to the County boundary just North of Monmouth.

The man in charge of the Traffic Department was Jim Walby, a man you could always talk to. He operated an 'open door' policy – a policy which others have since claimed to have invented. What I and many others liked about him, was that he always showed an interest, he always cared, and most importantly you always felt that you could trust him. Apart from being the boss, you knew that he would always try to keep you off the cross, and try to prevent others from nailing you up aloft.

In those far off days in Abergavenny, the areas of patrol, in their priority for motor cyclists were *Local*, which was a motor cyclist was always in a five to ten mile radius of Abergavenny, operating out as far as Penpergwm on the A40 Monmouth Road, up the A465 Heads of the Valleys Road to the County Boundary at Aberbaden, out along the A4042 road as far as Llanover, and up the A465 Hereford Road to the boundary at Llangua. This was a wide and interesting area to cover. Next was the A40 from Abergavenny to Dixton Road, Monmouth, then back down the A449 from Raglan to Caerleon. This was a nightmare wide load route, because it meant a journey against the one-way system at Caerleon when taking a load through Southbound. The next route for the motor cyclists was the A4042 Abergavenny to Pontypool road, but also covering Cwmbran and down as far as Llantarnam, and then finally the Valleys area, including all of Abertillery, Blackwood and Risca Divisions.

The Inspector in charge was another Welsh Rugby International star, R.T. Evans, a fair but no nonsense man. If you were due to finish at 5pm and he saw you in the Traffic Yard at twenty to the hour he sent you back out on patrol with a flea in your ear. The most senior sergeant was Reg Walbyoff, whose father many years before had been a Superintendent in the Force. Reg had obviously done some boxing in years gone by, as he had a distinctive cauliflower ear. I well remember the story of when he was out at Triley in the Landrover when the roads were almost impassable with snow. He stopped to assist a motorist, when a car ran into the back of his vehicle. He got out of the Landrover at the same time as the apologetic lady alighted from her car, and before he could say a word – because he clearly meant to, the lady took one look at him and the snow melted all around her. He was a man of few words, but you just had to like him. Ted Jones was the sergeant who normally wrote the duty rosters, so you had to keep in with him. A big man he had the most beautiful handwriting. The others were Frank Williams, who I had worked with earlier at Abergavenny station, and Eric Keegan, both of whom were totally fair minded.

I quickly learnt the best places to have a warm. This motor cycling business could be pretty awful in the rain, and whatever you had on, it never seemed to keep the water out. One of my favourite places to have a cup of coffee was the Milk Bar in Penpergwm, just next door to the Bryn Engineering garage. It was extremely convenient for the Local A40 and A4042 riders to meet and have a cup of coffee or tea. You turned the volume up on your radio on the bike, and put the handset through the window, so you could answer Headquarters if they called you without running back to the bike. Those were the days. That, however, presuming that the radio was working because they were notoriously unreliable. It seemed that wherever you went you had to ring in to see if there were any messages. If the radio

The Author on a B.S.A. 650cc Thunderbolt motor cycle in 1966.

25

was faulty you had to make the hundred mile round journey to the Home Office Wireless Depot at Bridgend, and having done so, the blessed thing could be U.S. before you got back to Abergavenny. But it was a pleasant day out.

It was most unusual for an officer with only twelve months service to be allowed to go on the motor cycle patrol, or it was in other forces. But Mike Wyatt had been on the bikes two months earlier than me and Mike Curr came on with under a years service, replacing Tony Eden who had gone on the cars and was soon to be stationed at Castleton covering the Cardiff Road.

Being so light, I had considerable difficulty in putting my Gold Flash on the main stand, there being no side stand as it had broken off some time before I had the machine. I was still on probation, and I was having difficulty in finding a way of booking anyone. It was to be almost three months before I perfected the system, and booked my first motorist. What he must have thought when I stopped him and asked him to hold my bike whilst I got my pocket book out, goodness only knows The problem was – this was how I survived as a motor cyclist for almost a year. Either the victim held my bike or I leaned it against the kerb or hedgerow.

Early in 1965 Mike Wyatt and I attended the Training Centre at Bridgend for two weeks to undertake our Intermediate Continuation course. We were doing really well, out of twenty students, I was eighteenth, whilst Mike was joint last with a Newport Borough man, John Davey. No one could believe that we were on the bikes, and we were the envy of many. It was not a very pleasant experience at our subsequent de-briefing on our return to Monmouthshire, but the big consolation as Inspector R.T. put it – we couldn't get any worse. And still I wasn't thrown off the Traffic.

Also, early in that year I attended the Glamorgan Constabulary's Driving School at Bridgend for a three week Standard Motor Cycle Course. There were four of us on the course, myself and three men from Glamorgan, of which Norman Abrahams, who owned a Standard Swallow, the forerunner of the Jaguar, stands out in my memory. The instructor was Dai Evans, a mature P.C. who could almost make a bike talk. The examiner was Sergeant John Webber. I recall two things as we travelled around South Wales, the first was when Dai came up alongside me on his more powerful machine, and managed to get his clutch lever stuck in my right hand gauntlet, and the frightening experience as he tried to free us. This he managed to do, and all without putting me on the deck, although my heart was racing, and I needed to stop for a fag to help me recover. The other point was that I put two marks on Norman on the final ride – I had 80 and he had 78.

Eventually the big day came, and three spanking new B.S.A. A65 650cc Thunderbolt motor cycles arrived in the garage via R.J. Ware and Sons of Newport, the dealer from which most of the bikes and spares came. Who was to have them? The A.J.S. that Tony Eden, and latterly Mike Curr had, was going, as was Mike Wyatt's and my Gold Flashes. I wasn't too bothered who had them, as long as I had one, and I quickly went down and picked one out, and hurriedly started polishing it. No one was going to get hold of mine – polish and all. In the event I had KAX 303D whilst the two Mikes had 301 and 302. These were fine machines, all white, fitted with leg shields but no farings. They even had something none of the previous bikes had, – blue flashing lights. We all three carefully ran them in, and come the day when they were all nicely bedded in took all three on the Hereford Road towards Pontrilas. We quickly found that their top speed was 104m.p.h., but had to come down in speed when all the bits and pieces so essential to the operation of the machines started to fall off – such was the vibration of those Beezers. They were nonetheless fine motor cycles, of which we were understandably proud, and woe betide anyone who rode mine when I was off.

At about this time I went back to Bridgend to undertake my Advanced Motor Cycle Course, and whilst I had the second highest mark out of the last four courses, there being three men on each, with 84, I still only achieved a Class 2 Certificate – I was heartbroken. The other two students were both from Cardiff City, and I look back with some amusement at how they improved my education. Johnny Tombs and John Williams would play Gin Rummy every night, and I watched with interest. After a day or so I asked if I could try my hand – I was on the hook. Yes, I could, but better, they said, if we just played a friendly – no money or anything. So there I was, and wasn't I good at it? That is until we started playing for cash, only small amounts, but I soon had none. They both had a Class 1 Certificate in Card Playing, whilst I, the gullible one, had failed convincingly.

The Police Forces in the United Kingdom had operated a Police Mobile column in the Summer months. This was around 50 – 100 men, who together

The Author with his Triumph 500cc motor cycle on the Police Mobile Column at Towyn in 1966.

Police Mobile Column vehicles – Austin Gypsy and Thames Trader Trucks.

The Police Mobile Column at Towyn in 1966.

with equipment, lorries, jeeps and motor cycles were almost self contained, and in the case of an emergency or other national disaster would be able to respond to assist the local populace. I remember that Mike Dixon drove the Monmouthshire contingent to Towyn in the North of Wales, where we were to be based. Arriving at about 6pm, it was found that the bikes – 350cc and 500cc Triumphs were in an appaling condition. We had to ride through the night to Merseyside to obtain spare parts, and on our return worked until dawn to get them roadworthy. That perhaps is an exaggeration – to get them so they would go. I had a 500cc bike with a 7 inch split in the exhaust, which for some reason used oil as fast as petrol. Every time we stopped after a 50 mile or so run, I had to replenish the oil. Better that, than ride in the back of a lorry and become a foot soldier.

The idea was that the bikes would ride ahead of the convoy, like Don-Rs and man the junctions to enable the convoy to move at speed, with safety, and indicate to the truck drivers the direction they were to go. The man would hold his arm up to show the direction, and after the convoy had passed would quickly overtake the convoy for the process to continue, we had great fun. It was like being at the Isle of Man T.T. Unfortunately one of our number leaned against a lamp-post in Dolgelli, and the whole convoy took the route indicated by his lazy arm, which needless to say was not the way they should go. Well we soon sorted it out and got them back on track. I remember on one occasion as I was making my way to the front, I had got my inside view, in readiness to overtake a truck driven by 'Big John' Williams, when he clipped a wall on the left, and I was showered with bricks flying past my head – but I survived.

We undertook a night exercise one day and I recall, as we returned to the Army Camp where we were billeted, a young sprogg of a service officer overtook in his sports car. He stopped, got out, and started ranting and raving at us. The Police Superintendent in charge of the convoy, unfortunately took his part, and thought he was going to put us straight as well. None of it, the Army officer had been drinking, and among our Police contingent were a couple of old soldiers, and they told the Superintendent that he was out of order, and if he didn't retract his comments they would have pleasure in arresting the army chap for drink driving – yes he had been drinking, or why else would he have tried to make a complete ass of himself. It was the first time I had ever seen a Senior Police officer climb down, and it was just as well that he did, as relations between the Police and Army would have been sorely strained. The young Army bloke went scurrying for cover, presumably to sleep it off – we didn't see his face again.

Part of the week involved travelling to another Army Camp at Rhyl. It was the height of the summer and if you remember was at the time when the 'Mods and Rockers' problem was upon us. Groups of youths, belonging to the two factions – those who rode scooters and those who rode real bikes – would descend on a Seaside Resort and thereafter would follow a series of pitched battles which put ordinary, decent folk in fear. It was a frightening period. Our arrival at the camp coincided with another outbreak of violence on the seafront at Rhyl and the local Police being woefully undermanned to cope called for assistance. A couple of trucks were quickly loaded with men from the Mobile Column and hurriedly sped to town. I understand that Rhyl didn't have trouble with Mods and Rockers for a number of years thereafter. The poor devils didn't know what had hit them. There were no injuries to the Police Officers, and I understand that no arrests were made, but the local Ambulance Service and hospitals were stretched to the limit that night.

Returning to Monmouthshire, Bob Hitchings and Mansel were soon to transfer to the cars, and were replaced by Phil Pritchard and Bob Daniels. Subsequently, these two were to have new B.S.A. Thunderbolts, LWO 120E and 121E. A modified specification which gave better road holding, they had a 4 inch rear wheel instead of the 3 inch, but a lower top speed.

Wide loads were a major part of our working day, and it was possible to spend upwards of a week without doing anything else. I remember escorting a wide and high load from Skenfrith up Trebella Pitch turning left for Newcastle and Rockfield, and then descending into Monmouth. Just past the entrance to the town, and travelling towards Raglan, the load caught the front of a terraced house on the left, causing a considerable amount of damage – most of the front of the building having fallen onto the pavement. I and the lorry driver and his crew were most apologetic to the dear little old lady who came to where the door had only a few minutes earlier been hanging. Surprisingly instead of being upset she appeared to be overjoyed. It transpired that she had been waiting for a long time for a Council house, and now she had to be rehoused immediately. She even made us tea and toast, whilst the man from the local Council surveyed the impossible situation and growled at us. We in the Monmouthshire Constabulary aimed to please.

The main abnormal load operator in South Wales was the Newport firm of Robert Wynn and Sons Ltd., who also had depots in Stafford, Manchester and Cardiff. This old established family business dated back to 1863 and they were known throughout the land. They even undertook contracts abroad in the desert, and in Nigeria. It was no surprise that when you were escorting the same vehicles on so many occasions that you got to know the drivers and their mates personally. When you were directed to escort a load, you would wonder who the crew was until you arrived at the boundary to pick them up. Wynns had some excellent kit – whilst they still had ex-Canadian Army Pacifics' and ex-U.S. Army Diamond Ts which had been continuously updated and rebuilt, they had an ever increasing fleet of Scammell Super Constructors and the like. Much of the heavy work was done with two tractors, push pull style, the vehicles being fitted with bell communication between units, so that indications of stop and go could be given. Many of their loads were in the region of 100 tons plus, and some of the equipment was so big and long that it had to be escorted even when empty.

I well recall picking a load up with another motor cyclist at the county boundary at Aberbaden on the Heads of the Valleys road, and finding that it was a huge bulldozer, the width was greater than it should have been, because the blade was still on it. I should have refused to move it until the blade was removed, but it was quiet, so we plodded on down to Hardwick Roundabout along the three lane road, and then without difficulty along the A40 towards

Raglan. We had done it all before, and we knew exactly where to stop the traffic to ensure the safety of the public. From Raglan we pulled into Reg Watkin's garage where the Wynn's driver refuelled, taking on about 100 gallons of diesel, not an unwelcome sight for Mr. Watkins who also ran an excellent transport cafe, and then on our way again, having been refreshed by tea and toast, all on the driver. We got to Mitchell Troy just as light was fading and laid the load up overnight, arranging with the driver Ian Trick, to pick him up the following morning at eight. It would take two of us as the load was due to go up towards Coleford to a place called Yorkley in Gloucestershire, and the road uphill from Monmouth towards the county boundary at Staunton was pretty narrow and very winding.

Next morning, a Sunday, I was in work for seven, and was met by Sergeant Ted Jones who wanted me to do this load on my own, and my mate to do another from Glangrwney. I dare not tell him the load due to go up over Staunton needed two of us, so I just rode out to Mitchell Troy to find Ian Trick reconnecting his unit, having travelled back from his home at Newport. He was surprised to see me alone, but I'd done it before, and it was early and a Sunday, it should be pretty quiet, with hopefully little traffic. We set off, I kept the road clear and stopped the traffic at the widest points. As we travelled, my mind wandered to when I would have to pass it over to my counterpart in Gloucestershire, although as yet I had not given an E.T.A. I suddenly thought, what if he's an awkward devil. I had never been to Yorkley, I didn't know where it was, but I was determined to find out. I radioed to Headquarters that the loads ultimate destination was only about a mile inside Gloucestershire, and to save that constabulary sending anyone out to finish it for such a short distance I'd pop it there. We often did this for each other, with surrounding forces. The trouble was that Yorkley was a hell of a distance from the boundary, but they thankfully, for me, accepted the offer. The journey on from Staunton turned into a nightmare, the road got ever increasingly more winding, narrower, steeper, and at times the offending bulldozer blade was gouging out whole mounds of banking as we struggled on. At last we arrived at our Forest of Dean destination, where I sat down on the verge, wiped my sweating brow, lit a cigarette and reflected on my narrow escape from unemployment.

Pickfords too, were much in evidence. I once picked up a heavy, wide and high load at Skenfrith. It was manned by an experienced crew from Sheffield. Well it took a day to get it over the river bridge at Skenfrith, the boggies had to be reversed and a fair amount of jacking had to be done. Having got over the bridge, and with fading light it was going to be unsafe to proceed further that evening, and anyhow the diversions had been stood down. I just got the driver to shove it into the entrance to the village alongside the green. Unfortunately movement into and out of the village that night had to be via the green, which was steep and bumpy, and many phone calls of complaint were received at Headquarters. But no one was hurt. The next day was spent plodding towards Abergavenny – it was routed all the way along the Ross Road, to its junction with Hereford Road, then round the Angel Corner in Abergavenny destined to continue further south.

31

The problem manifested itself when we got to the railway bridge just past Maindiff Court Hospital. The load wouldn't go under. It was routed that way, but the offending load being a steel vessel, had a two inch flange which stopped its further movement. So that night the load was left well signed, blocking a whole lane by the bridge. Well the road wasn't too busy, was it? The next morning engineers turned up from Pickfords in Cardiff and took the offending flange off with a torch. Continuing on day 3 we managed to get it round the corner at the junction with Ross Road, into Hereford Road, and then down to the Angel Corner. Of course it wouldn't go round, until part of the Electricity Board shop and the Great George Hotel had been re-designed. Eventually we drew into the Bus Station, where the Yorkshireman who was in charge of the outfit just about exploded. End of day 3. The next day we got rid of it at the boundary with Newport Borough Police at Llantarnam. Thank goodness!

On another occasion I was escorting a Heanor haulage load along the high load route from Grosmont towards Cross Ash, when we encountered the last steep hill before reaching the village. It was a Saturday, and the previous day the Council had resurfaced the road at this point. It was a hot, sticky day, and the wet tar had melted like treacle. It took all the ingenuity of Cyril Lane of W.G. Lane and Sons, and his two heavy breakdown trucks to get the load up the hill. Needless to say there was an awful lot of paperwork concerning the tarmac which had to be relaid. It wasn't my fault.

Reflecting back, when I went on the bikes there was very little dual carriageway in the County. Just a short strip by British Nylon Spinners at Mamhilad, and another at Forge Lane. On April 9, 1965, the big occasion arrived, and the Croesyceiliog Bye-pass was opened. It was a nightmare, drivers had little or no experience of dual carriageways, even though it was a major step forward in the road network in the County. You had cars going north on the southbound carriageway and others going south on the northbound lanes. And at the same time you had others with more sense trying to use the correct carriageways. After a day or two of gentle advice, it was no good I had to get my 'naughty' book out – they soon learnt.

The Courts were interesting. There was even a court at Cross Ash alongside the Police Station, and once a month on a Saturday morning, Bill Hughes who was the local Bobby and his wife Nan would provide tea for Magistrates, Clerk, Defendants and Police alike, irrespective of their station in life. I liked Bill and his wife, they were always glad to see us when we patrolled out their way, and the kettle was soon on.

One Wednesday morning of the 44 cases on the Court Register at Abergavenny, I had 42 of them. All concerned the siting of a 'No Right Turn' sign on the Heads of the Valleys Road at Llanfoist. When the sign was put up no one took any notice of it, so one morning I was sent, alone, to sort it out. I quickly had a queue of culprits to book, and before long they were queueing in the centre lane, actually waiting to commit the offence. My how my hand ached. Whilst on the subject of this sign, on one occasion I booked a well-known Welsh Rugby International the very day that he was moving north to Salford – and on my return to Headquarters late that day, my radio being faulty, I was met by a whole bevy of senior officers, from Detective

Superintendent down, and they didn't take kindly to knowing that my sport was snooker. No matter my shoulders were broad, or they were with Jim Walby, the boss backing me up. – Bless him.

One of Abergavenny's most beautiful landmarks was the Sugar Loaf mountain, and on a Summer's day there was no nicer experience than riding to the very top, and parking the bike, whilst one enjoyed a cigarette or one's sandwiches, picnic style. Well that was fine, so we thought. A week or two later the National Park Warden for the Brecon Beacons approached the boss and asked if we could patrol the area to stop young boys riding their motor bikes up there. What had we done? Having started the craze, we now had official sanction to try and stop it.

Once a week a dance was held at Llanarth Club, and being single, I decided to go. I drove my car, my brand new Morris Minor 1000, parked it out of harms way, and went into the club to enjoy myself. Some of the Abergavenny unmentionables quickly singled me out. I felt distinctly uncomfortable. I was a Police Officer, I couldn't get involved in a fracas. Anyway four or five of them came up to me looking for trouble, being a bit worse for drink, and at that moment I heard a voice behind me, and saw Ray Hockey standing there. Ray, who at that time worked for Lanes had driven the coach out from Abergavenny as he did every week with the youngsters who attended. Well Ray wasn't having any of it. If they wanted to take Paul Heaton on, an off duty Paul Heaton, they had to take Ray Hockey on. Anyway with my courage restored, for I was no longer alone, the two of us threw five of them out of the club. We being sober. Thank you Ray. He subsequently came to work in the Headquarters Workshop.

Meanwhile my proficiency as a Police Constable had improved. I was reporting my fair share of offenders, it must be said mostly for the Road Traffic related transgressions, but I also arrested a number of youths in stolen cars. One such arrest, was as the result of an officer travelling towards Abergavenny from Risca to have his vehicle serviced, sighting the vehicle, a Hillman Minx, also approaching the town. On his arrival at Headquarters he circulated the information, and I set out immediately in search. I did not have to look long, as I had only travelled the short distance from Monk Street towards the Bus Station, when the vehicle started to pull out from the left. I was late noticing it, and he actually managed to turn into the flow of traffic travelling behind me. Once he realised that I had seen him, he turned into Fosterville Crescent with me turning a sharp left in pursuit. Within fifty yards he ran the car into a tree and jumped out, legging it on foot over gardens towards the Monmouth road. I would never have had time to put my bike on its stand, I just dropped it on the ground, didn't switch the engine off or anything. Just took off after him, so great was the prize. Alas, when I got to the wall that he had just jumped over without looking, I being a much more cautious individual, looked before I was prepared to leap. It was as I suspected a long way down. He being obviously a very athletic type, who I subsequently learned played rugby at club level, had no problems, and I saw him disappearing down Mill Street. I retraced my steps, returned to my machine, the engine of which had by now stalled. I transmitted the direction of travel of our Olympic hero to Operations Room, and returned to Headquarters to replenish my bike's petrol and oil, which had been spilt over the road at the point of disembarkation.

Thereafter around a dozen Police Officers tried to seal off that area to which he, the culprit had last been seen running. I rode my motor cycle up alongside the Castle wall, and looked across the Castle Meadow. Sure enough in the distance I saw him trying to get away. Unfortunately, he soon dropped from sight, and gradually the search for him was scaled down.

However, I wasn't giving up – not just yet. After about two hours without a sighting of the culprit I began to despair of catching him. I had covered the entire outer area of where I had last seen him, and had just parked my bike at the bottom of the Heads of the Valleys Road, and was looking towards the Castle Meadow from the small lay-by near Hardwick, when behind me I heard a screech of brakes. I looked around and saw a lorry coming to a halt on the opposite side of the road, and our villain jumping out of the passenger side of the cab. He tore off at speed up the bank and through the hedge – he wasn't going to get away this time, I thought. I came down over the bank of the farmland just in time to see him enter a barn at the bottom. This boy could run. I went straight up to the entrance and dismounted, shouting to him that all was up. He quietly came out, exhausted, and gave himself up. He was too knackered to even speak. I radioed for transport and he was soon on his way to Abergavenny Police Station. It transpired that he had stolen the car from Newport, and the Police there soon sent an escort to claim him. Many years later I met this young chap and recognised him immediately. He had turned out well considering his start, and I quite liked him. I told him that when he was in the lorry all those years earlier, if he hadn't panicked, I would never have seen him, and he would probably never have been caught. We laughed.

Once we were carrying out some spring cleaning at the Traffic Yard office. Inspector Roy Smallcombe offered to take me round to Richards' shop in Frogmore Street, to get some paint. On arrival I went in to pick it up whilst he remained in the car outside, with the engine running. Not usually clumsy, I must have caught a glimpse of a young lady, as on my way out of the shop I tripped. The paint went everywhere, over the window, pavement and door. I looked up, just in time to see the Police Westminster disappearing down the street like a getaway car leaving the scene of a crime where a co-conspirator had been caught. Happily the staff of the shop helped me clean the mess, they being that kind of people. Cleaned up, I was soon on my way in pursuit of and to confront my getaway driver. I always knew I'd get my own back.

During 1966 one of the saddest events in my living memory occurred at the village of Aberfan. So many children and their teachers were lost that tragic Thursday morning. Much has been written about Aberfan, and what happened at that tiny valley village will never be forgotten. I know because I saw for myself when I was directed there with an important piece of earth-moving equipment which had been rushed at top speed from the Midlands under continuous escort. I will never forget. How could I.

Farewell Monmouthshire, Hello Gwent

On August 31, 1964 the Chief Constable of Monmouthshire, Mr. Neil Galbraith stood down from his post on his appointment as one of Her Majesty's Inspectors of Constabulary. This was a most important post, and we the men and women of his force were justly proud. Mr. Farley who had been his Assistant, was duly appointed taking up the post from September 1. William Farley was a man who had a military background, and looked most distinguished with his dark hair and moustache. Although our leader had changed, I was still part of the same family – and felt happy about it. A kindly man, Mr. Drury, became the Assistant Chief Constable.

However, on April 1, 1967 under directives from the Home Office, and in accordance with the provisions of the Police Act, the Monmouthshire Constabulary was amalgamated with the Newport Borough Police Force, which was thereafter restyled as the Gwent Constabulary. Mr. Farley became the new Chief Constable, and Mr. Frank Smead the Chief Constable of Newport became the Deputy Chief of the new force. Mr. Drury was appointed as A.C.C.

Towards the end of March 1967 I had spent a few weeks in the Operations Room at Headquarters, filling in for those who were away on courses, leave or sickness, and by the end of the month I was really getting to like it. No rain, no wind, no wettings, plenty of tea, and not too much pressure. I was assisting the Operations Room sergeant and his small staff of ladies in the important function of directing the force. Yes, I can say I was really enjoying this, and thought it might not be a bad idea to try and stay. I had let this fact become known – and 'yes' they thought it a good idea too. But, thankfully as things turned out, no firm decision had been made. Come the 1st of April, the day of the amalgamation, and known for some other reason which quite escapes me at the moment, the workload from the former Newport Borough force was channelled through the Operations Room at Abergavenny in addition to that generated by the old five former Monmouthshire Divisions. Suddenly Ops. Room was not such a warm comfortable place to be. Pressure there was a plenty. Tea – you didn't have time to put the kettle on let alone take a meal break. The thought of wind, rain and a wet backside was, suddenly, not so bad after all. How the hell was I going to get out of there. As luck would have it, my bike was still up in the yard – no one had replaced me. Mr. Walby, I knew always passed through the corridor at 8am sharp each morning, and I just happened to be on his route on this particular day, lying in wait for him as it were. Always a gentleman, he asked how I was getting on – to which I replied how much I was missing the bikes. I didn't say how much I was missing the wide open spaces, the Milk Bar at Penpergwm, Reg Watkins' at Raglan, Ma Lumley's in Raglan village and the Yat Cafe. No that wouldn't have sounded right. To my relief he said, "Yes you've been in there long enough, time to get you back out". I don't think I was fooling him, but he was a good judge of character – he could recognise a cry for help when he heard one. And so it was after a few days I emerged back in the Traffic Yard – a Motor Cyclist again. Even Harry Winney the handyman laughed about my escape.

During my absence Mike Wyatt had gone on the cars, being partnered with Bob MacDowall. It was Mike's dream come true, what he really wanted, AND with a partner most would have killed to have. His place had been taken by Bryan Knight who had come from Tredegar. Well Bryan was a compulsive worker, not a trait which I had hitherto been wholeheartedly known for, and I could see how good he was looking, and how bad the rest of us were looking. We tried everything to slow him down – Coventry, quiet little chats, even arranged more than his fair share of wide loads – but he could pot a few on his way to start the escort. It was clear that gone were our comfortable days – there was only one thing for it, we couldn't beat him, so reluctantly we had to join him. After the initial shock we got used to it and even began to like it. It says much for Bryan's character – and he really was an excellent Policeman. We soon became firm friends,. Alf Trumper, who was on patrol at Pontypool, before transferring to become the Chief's Chauffeur, was always taking the 'mickey' used to call us 'Stan and Olly', as Bryan was much bigger than I and I had an unfortunate habit of scratching the

P.C. Bryan Knight with B.S.A. 650cc motor cycles at the Traffic Yard, Police Headquarters, Abergavenny in 1968.

top of my head when I took my crash helmet off.

We were issued with breeches and leggings, and I had the marvellous idea of buying a pair of War Department Despatch Rider's boots. I really looked the 'kiddy' in these. The only thing, they had to be laced up all the way to the top, and when mounting the bike, they being so heavy – and me so light, I had to practically lift my leg over with both hands. This continued for a few days, until on one particularly hot summer day I was chasing after a couple of female absconders at Mitchell Troy, which necessitated leaving my bike at the side of the road and running up a steep field. By the time I reached the top I was on all fours, just in time to see the local Bobby, Arthur Millett collar them, he being at least twenty years my senior and barely out of breath. On my return to Headquarters the offending lead weights were consigned to the bin, and that was how I became known as "Bootsie".

Abnormal loads continued to fill a lot of the motor cyclists' day, and during this period we were inundated with loads enroute to Aberthaw Power Station. Whole fleets of lorries left Glasgow daily laden with elements, which had a width of 14 feet, but unfortunately on the journey south the convoys of five or six lorries would become separated from each other. So that early in the morning, you would pick up two or three loads at the Yat Cafe, escort them to Caerleon, and no sooner had you finished with those than a couple more were laid up at the Yat waiting to make the journey, and so on. It was not impossible to make this journey up to four times a day. So much mileage was being covered that I often had to buy petrol to enable me to finish the job. I obviously got the money back at Headquarters.

One driver with a speech impediment, would arrive at the boundary and telephone to Headquarters asking for an escort and unfortunately in getting the words out often kicked the bottom pane of glass out of the kiosk. Unfortunately one day he turned up at the boundary with a high load, which necessitated the attendance of the Post Office Telephone and Electricity Board engineers to accompany the load to lift the phone and electric wires to enable it to pass under. On this occasion the driver, a lovely chap, stopped to contact his firm. We were all enjoying a cigarette and a short break, when we heard the sound of breaking glass, and the G.P.O. too had discovered the identity of the culprit. They had some difficulty previously in working out why it was just the bottom panes of glass which were being vandalised. I admit – we knew all along.

One of Wynn's drivers, Billy Wade, of Usk, turned up with the first of twelve steel vessels enroute from Manchester to Cardiff Gas Works. All went well until we were negotiating the Jockey Pitch at Pontypool, when suddenly the load slipped from the front boggie, dropped to the ground and ran back for about fifty yards before coming to a halt. The wire hawsers holding it on the boggie had parted. It was indeed fortunate that I had gone to the top of the hill, as was my usual practice and called all the following traffic from behind it. I had known Billy for years, but it didn't matter he had to go in the 'naughty' book, and he knew it. Subsequently I attended and reported the firm for the insecure load as well. But to their credit, they expressed their appreciation of my efforts when pleading guilty before Pontypool Magistrates

The Author at the Traffic Yard, Abergavenny in 1968, preparing motor cycles for a V.I.P. visit.

The Author at the scene of a road accident at Hardwick Roundabout, Abergavenny in 1968.

Court. So heavy did Wynn's solicitor lay it on, that I finished up receiving a Commendation from the Magistrates. I recall the headlines in the local paper – 'Police Officer Averts Disaster', and the next time I saw Billy Wade, he asked if he could be my agent.

Inspector R.T. Evans had long since been promoted, and a number of other bosses had followed – Inspectors Tom O'Connell, Roy Smallcombe and Fred Wyer. The sergeants had changed too, gone were Frank Williams and Eric Keegan on promotion, and Terry Jayne and Len Reynolds together with Ken Gardner had arrived. At about this time Mr. Smallcombe decided that I should take the step from motor cycle to patrol car, and I was sent to Cwmbran where I was teamed up with 'Big' John Williams. He was a great guy, and we had some fun – and we did some good work together, but I missed the bikes and Superintendent Walby allowed me to go back. I appreciated this. I was I'm sure the only officer who ever willingly went back. I had got used to the rain soaked kit and missed it. The truth, if it be told, was that I was in fact a loner. I liked to do it my way, and in a patrol car with someone else, he might turn left, when I wanted to go right.

By this time Mike Wyatt had a new mate on the cars, Constable David Jones, whose father was a sergeant in the Mid Wales Police. I liked Dai, he was a gentle giant with a truly kindly disposition. One day whilst he was out on his own he clouted his patrol car, a Ford Zephyr, Mk. 2, Index KAX 870D, and having a brother in the trade had almost got it fixed before the radio summoned him back to see the sergeant. The job was excellent, and if he had had another fifteen minutes the paint would have set, but unfortunately it showed a few runs. Talk your way out of that Dai. Like a Man, he took his medicine – but Uncle Jim Walby, the boss, knew a good one when he saw one, and Dai stayed. David went to West Mercia on promotion some years later, and unfortunately was cut down in the prime of his life. Sadly I was a bearer at his funeral.

Talk to Bryan Knight today, and if he remembers any one incident concerning me, it will surely be me chasing after birds. We were travelling up the Heads of the Valleys Road, having just set off from Hardwick Roundabout, Abergavenny, when I ran straight flat bang into a crow. I stopped, as if hit by a sledge, my lungs having been emptied of air involuntarily. I couldn't get my breath, I couldn't put the bike on the stand I was completely winded for over a minute or two. Bryan saw the seriousness of the situation, but I could still see him stifling a chuckle. The crow was stone dead. It was a hell of an experience. We did not at that time have farings fitted to our machines. That slowed me down, for a bit.

On another occasion, it was in fact Boxing Day, and snow was on the ground, Ted Jones was the sergeant, and because of the bad weather, Bryan Knight, Phil Pritchard and myself were unable to use the bikes, and had been pressed into clearing the snow from the yard with shovels. As we did so, the sergeant called that there was a bad accident at Llangibby, and those in the Southern Traffic area could not get through. He wanted to send two of us in a Landrover. One was to stay, we tossed – Bryan – heads, Phil – heads, Paul – tails. They went, I stayed – shovel still in hand. Some while later I heard the

An insecure load at the Jockey Pitch, Pontypool in 1968. A large steel vessel being carried on an outfit owned by Robert Wynn and Sons Ltd., Newport, became detached and ran part way back down the hill. The drawing vehicle was a Diamond T, index No. 1300 DW.

radio report from them 'Triple fatal, car and milk lorry, Llangibby, main road'. Two short straws, one long.

I remember a similar thing had happened with Mike Wyatt. I had gone out to escort a Wynn's load from Abergavenny Bus Station early one morning, enroute towards the Yat, and having a faulty radio, went into Monmouth Police Station to report by telephone some hours later, to be told that Mike was dealing with a double fatal on the Heads of the Valleys, and I had been completely oblivious to it. I must have actually been only about a mile from the accident when it happened, as at about that moment I was turning up towards Raglan in front of a Diamond T.

I know that others will dispute this. The distance from Raglan to Abergavenny is nine miles on what is now the old road. The fastest of Robert Wynn and Sons drivers was Ian Trick, and he held the record from Abergavenny (Hardwick Roundabout) to the Raglan By-pass of 21 minutes, and 19 minutes in the opposite direction. This was with a 100 ton plus outfit, and with a tractor at both ends. His being a Scammell Super Constructor, index number GDW 231D. I know because I escorted him in both directions. Ian subsequently left Wynns and set himself up in business at Newport trading as Kerricabs.

It was most unusual for Police Officers to own their own homes. How could we afford to, as we were at that time so poorly paid. Anyway, we could be required to move at a moments notice to another station or division on the other side of the Force area, which entailed uprooting family with what all that entailed – new schools for the children, a wife who if working had to give notice and try to find other employment near to the new home. As a result the Constabulary at that time owned a considerable number of Police houses. All of which were occupied, and to obtain such a civilised roof over one's head was more difficult than panning for gold. I had been courting for some time, and it was always a worry to me that if I was to get married, this would entail having to find accommodation which might not be up to the standard that I and my prospective bride were used to. My wife to be Gill had a young son by a previous marriage, and it was totally impractical for us to live in some flat in the town probably situated over a shop premises, as so many young couples were.

I had kept our courtship to myself, and we decided to buy a house in New Inn, in the village where I had been brought up, and not far from where Gill lived. In view of all the circumstances, and because she was a nursing sister earning considerably more than I, the property was put in her name; she obtained a mortgage without any difficulty. As I recall we took possession of the house on the Tuesday, commenced decorating, bought furniture, and quickly got things ship shape as it were. All through this short period we stayed at our respective homes, as was right and proper. Come the Friday of that week I turned up at Headquarters with an already completed application form, stating that I was getting married on the Monday and applying for permission to live at the new address – a house owned by my wife to be. I conveniently omitted to say that she had only owned it for three days or so. There were no limits to the lengths I would go to get my own way. My

41

application was studied apparently in some detail, and someone unkindly, but conveniently for me, made the assertion that 'I had to get married'. It was in this way that I became virtually the first officer in the county with under twenty-five years service to obtain his own home, I at that time still being something of a sprog with only a little over fours years completed. Happily the wedding took place, my colleagues studied the photographs in great detail, and imagine everyone's delight and surprise when our daughter Jane was born at the County Hospital, Panteg, fifteen months later.

One day I had to attend at Ebbw Vale Magistrates' Court to give evidence. This day was like no other I had experienced, as on arrival half an hour early it was impossible not to notice that just about every room in the Police Station, enquiry office, cells, cell passage, canteen, offices, and even the toilets were full of people who had apparently been relieved of their liberty. At that time the force had two officers, a sergeant and a constable, stationed at the Ebbw Vale steelworks, and whilst I do not accurately know the full details, there was some allegation that material – principally scrap metal, was being weighed in at the gate – twice. In other words, weighed twice and actually delivered once. The subsequent investigation hung over the force like a cloud, but the officer who was alleged to have been at the centre of things, John Enoch, was never convicted of any offence to my knowledge, even though a number of trials followed and died with an unblemished character.

Preparations for the Investiture of Prince Charles as the Prince of Wales on July 1, 1969 at Caernarfon, called for a number of Gwent men to go north to assist. The requirement as far as the Traffic Department was concerned was for motor cyclists on small machines. This entailed the calling in of all the forces' 350cc outstation motor cycles, and a hell of a lot of hard work to get them gleaming and up to scratch. Come the days prior to the Investiture itself our contingent of well qualified riders set out north followed by the motor cycle fitter John Hayward in a Landrover and trailer together with a spare machine and all the kit required to keep them running. My daughter, being expected on the day itself – meant that I was to stay behind, and was employed on getting the big machines, the patrol bikes – the 650s all spick and span. In readiness for the return of my colleagues from North Wales, when we would all be required to escort His Highness on that part of the Principality which went through our area on his long tour of Wales. It was a lovely day, everyone, the public, were marvellous, and wherever you went you saw children waving and street parties. It was a day always to be remembered.

In the history of the force, whilst most motor cyclists had attended Standard and Advanced Courses at Bridgend, no one had ever undertaken a Refresher Course. I was still smarting at my Class 2 Certificate, and persuaded Sergeant Arthur Roynon, that most influential of persons on our department to put a good word in for me with Mr. Walby. Yes that would be alright. Thus I attended at Bridgend for my two weeks tuition where I was in the capable hands of Sergeant Cliff Thomas. The other two students were from other forces, an older chap with a Class 1 from Pembrokeshire, and a man about my age from Gwynedd. All went well until our West Walian came

Gwent Police Officers at Abergavenny with their Matchless 350cc motor cycles just prior to departure for Caernarfon for the Investiture of the Prince of Wales on July 1, 1969.

P.C.s Bryan Knight (left), Ron Eagle, John Bowditch, John McCarthy, Graham Jones, Bob Daniels, Mike Wyatt and Phil Pritchard.

off and injured himself on the Tuesday, whilst we were undertaking that most exacting of training on loose surfaces at Kenfig Sands. Soon comfortably tucked up in his hospital bed, the course continued, Cliff being ever watchful of our progress, and safety. Unfortunately, lightening does strike twice, for on the morrow, the man from North Wales lost control going around a left hand bend. We had only just come out from sheltering in a bus shelter, and there was considerable surface water in evidence. He was lucky, the bike missed some boulders on the side of the road, which was in fact common land, and came to rest about twenty yards further on in some reeds. The badly shaken rider had managed to continue on a further five or so yards bike-less as it were. He wasn't badly injured, neither of them had been, and they must have had a lot to talk about from their hospital beds conveniently situated next to each other. After that Cliff, who was now under a lot of pressure tried to wrap me in cotton wool. No one would ever believe it if I didn't complete the course either. Every morning he would ride down the drive from the Traffic Department followed by a solitary rider – me. And every time we returned a crowd of fitters would rush out from the workshops to see if I was still around – much money changing hands on their sighting of me.

Subsequently I finished the course, intact, and with a healthy 86 for survival. I had my Class 1 at last. Tragically in 1974 Cliff Thomas was killed in a motor cycle accident up towards Brecon, whilst instructing an Advanced Course. He is remembered.

I had passed my Promotion Examination to Sergeant in Educational Subjects way back in 1965, and the need for that exam was soon done away with. However, I had entered for my Sergeant's Exam in law subjects, on a couple of occasions, and enjoying life had withdrawn. One day I went into work, and Sergeant Terry Jayne, knowing that I was considering pulling out yet again, set me up. Mike Curr had passed six months earlier, and he mused as to how I was going to feel when Mike took over what he considered would be the newly created post of Motor Cycle Sergeant. The thought didn't bear thinking about. I was the senior man, if anyone should get that job it should be me. Our pay was poor, and promotion was the only way an officer could improve his financial position, and more importantly the standard of living of his family. Did Terry Jayne think I could pass? Oh yes. I quickly enrolled for a correspondence course with the School of Careers, and such was my feeling of urgency that I completed the whole thing in eight weeks, the normal period should have been over a year or more. Come the day of our practice exam at Pontypool Police Station, I came out of the room at the end of the day, to hear others giving their views as to the answers, and left for home feeling completely depressed and dejected, as those weren't the answers I had given. When the marks were released it was a different tale – I was at or near the top. I was upset when the Training Department asserted that my achievement had been a mere fluke.

The day of the exam proper, I attended at Allt-yr-yn Tech. where all 89 of us got down to the papers. I returned home – "no, if I haven't passed I'm not going through that again". That was my character, I'm too lazy to do anything twice. Come the results – twenty passed out of 89 – I was third in

Gwent; obviously another fluke.

Fifteen months later I passed the Inspector's examination, only this time I had dropped to seventh position, of those who sat from the Force.

Early in 1970 I attended in front of the Chief Constable, Mr. Farley for my Promotion Board. He was sitting with representatives of the Superintendents' Association and the Police Federation. I had to start by giving some account of myself. I said, hoping to break the ice, as they all looked very stern, that I had worked at Woolworths in Pontypool as a boy – and that I had been the original 'wonder of Woolies'. Not a smile. Well if I had intended to show my leader that I was the best thing since sliced bread, he didn't intend opening the wrapper. I went nowhere.

Well that's not quite correct, soon after I was put back on the patrol cars at Cwmbran. My partner this time was Tony Eden, with whom I had been on the bikes years earlier. He was a great guy. Work – he never stopped. Whatever we touched turned into collars. Arrests galore. Trouble was, on occasions I had just got out of the car to stop and talk to a driver when the offender would speed off. On one occasion I pursued on foot in a narrow lane behind some houses in Griffithstown – but I caught him. On another occasion the driver of a Mini van took off up Coedygric Road in the same village with me hanging on, just like a fool. But stop he did, when the door glass clouted him round the ear.

Years later, when lecturing to young recruits, I related the one incident that I still feel the greatest shame about. That concerned a coal-picker. All the coal over the hills belongs to the National Coal Board and no one has the right to remove it, even where it is not being mined – in fact it is an offence called theft. On this sunny afternoon I saw a chap in an Austin Cambridge, an old model well down at the rear just driving off the mountainside. He was accompanied by his wife, two kids and his mother-in-law. On opening the boot it was found to be full of coal which he and his had picked out. I booked him, and when he went to Court – he was given an Absolute Discharge. However, I was wrong, no matter what the law said, he was a man of limited means. I should have known better and on reflection should have been helping him to pick it, not booking him. That is my story to recruits. Make sure that you don't do things which you later regret as being small minded. Use your discretion.

Tony Eden and I used to pick up another driver, off the following shift from his home and drop him off at work. When we called in the darkness of night, he came out closed his back door and was invariably wearing sun glasses. There's nothing like being prepared for daylight, is there?

After six months on the patrol cars at Cwmbran I yearned to be back on the motor bikes at Abergavenny. Never known up till then, for my heavy weight, I was suddenly losing even more, which I could ill afford to do. I visited the doctor, but it wasn't really physical. I wasn't happy. I was a loner, always had been, and working in a patrol car I felt like a caged bird. Something had to be done. I saw Mr. Walby, who even spoke to my doctor, and they agreed that I would not be able to stay on the cars. I was overjoyed when my boss declared that I could go back on the motor cycles. Things had changed but I was back. It's more or less all I wanted. If it wasn't for the poor pay I would have been quite content to have finished my service as a motor cyclist. Riding on two wheels is like no other feeling on earth, and being paid to do so was doubly so.

Three of the boys who had come on the motor cycles after me, had transferred onto the cars, they were Bob Daniels, Phil Pritchard and Mike Curr. Replacing them were Keri Rowland, Dick Jones and Mike Gunter. Of course Bryan Knight was still there. When I returned I found that Dick had taken over my old bike, a B.S.A. 650cc Thunderbolt, index UAX 142H, and he being quite happy with this, I took over a new one, also a Beezer, WAX 735J.

In the late 1960s Mr Drury, the Assistant Chief Constable retired. His post had been advertised in the Police Review, and interviews undertaken at Abergavenny on one dull overcast day. The successful applicant was a sharp well presented Lancastrian – John Woodcock and I was probably the first Gwent constable he met, as I was the one in the Traffic yard at the very moment that a driver was required to convey him to Doctor Jordan's surgery for his medical. There was nothing stand offish about this man – even I could recognise someone who was going places. Even on that short journey he put me completely at ease, he was clearly a man who could relate to one and all, no matter what the 'station'. I liked him. On my return to the Traffic Yard, I was met with a barrage of questions, but instead of giving my true impressions – I told the boys that here was someone who was going to sort them out, someone whose middle name began with the letter B. A man like Judge Jefferys, a hanging and flogging merchant. Oh, how I upset them all. When Mr. Smead subsequently retired as Deputy Chief, Mr. Woodcock was promoted in his place, and the A.C.C.'s job was filled by Peter Palastanga from West Mercia, a tall individual who looked every bit a policeman.

Meanwhile life went on. I was travelling home from Abergavenny in my car at the end of a shift, when I was flagged down near Llanover by a motorist. A gentleman out with his wife had died in his car at the roadside. Apparently he had been terminally ill with lung cancer, and whilst his death was not entirely unexpected, it was still very sudden when it happened. Les Davies, a Training Department sergeant had also stopped, and we placed the deceased in the ambulance and did all we could for the widow, prior to the arrival of 'on duty' officers. All this done, Les, who like myself was a smoker, offered me a cigarette. It wasn't the fact that we had just dealt with a lung cancer victim, or the cigarette – it was the fact that instead of offering me the packet, he had put his fingers in to take one out, and blood dropped onto them. I couldn't look at a cigarette for nine months let alone smoke one.

As a Police Officer it was not uncommon to deal with the deaths of people from all manner of causes. In cases of 'Sudden Death' where the deceased's own doctor could not certify the cause of death, a post mortem resulted to establish the exact cause, and in all cases the Coroner was informed and a report compiled. Way back in my short period on the beat I had been sent to deal with three sudden deaths in as many days. It was the practice of getting young officers used to this aspect of the work earlier rather than later – a sensible course. Doctor Andrews, the Pathologist, would attend, and assisted by the Mortuary Attendant, would do the necessary. I am certainly not going into details, but it was normal practice for a Police Officer to be present, and at the conclusion payment made direct to the pathologist – £6.5s.0d in 1964, of which Doctor Andrews would give you five shillings if you were lucky. At the conclusion of my first post mortem I returned to the station for lunch, and having sat down opened my lunchbox where I found that Spam was on the menu. I quickly consigned my food to the bin, and for the next thirty years never took meat sandwiches to work again. Cheese would do nicely.

I had a fairly good record for staying in an upright position on my motor cycle. It was a matter of pride. If I did accidentally drop the bike, I straightened the bent areas out myself, and if beyond repair, paid out of my own pocket for the replacement parts, whatever they cost. One thing was sure – I kept my mouth shut – there was no limit to my deceit in this respect, and for my thirty years in the job, it cost me to keep my accident free record. I recall one incident when I received gravel rash was at Rockhill Road, Pontymoile. They had just redesigned the road, and introduced a one way system, with my former workplace – the Clarence Trading Company's premises in the middle. The new road had only been open for two days, and we had just had a very heavy downpour of rain. I remember, I travelled down Rockhill Road intending to turn left for Usk Road, and at the corner, the road being like an ice rink, with grease everywhere, the bike just slipped from under me. We arrived on the deck in an unceremonious heap. Just at that moment a Western Welsh double-decker bus turned up at the junction from the direction of New Inn. As the passengers in the top deck crammed to the offside windows to see this idiot on the floor I feared that the bus would topple on to me. In shock, instead of a face as white as a ghost, it was beetroot red, such was my embarrassment. Anyway I picked myself up off the floor, lifted the heavy bike – which I put on the side stand. Feeling that I ought to leave the large group of amused spectators I started the bike, jumped on, and set course towards Pontypool. Still dazed I heard behind me a public address system shouting – lift your stand up. Chief Inspector Roy Smallcombe had driven up behind me, and not knowing I'd just got up off the deck, noticed that my side stand was down. I put it up, and as directed followed him to Pontypool Police Station to confer. I followed, wondering how this little incident was going to go undetected, the nearside of the bike being somewhat buckled and bent. As Mr. Smallcombe parked his car to the rear of the Police Station, alighted, and walked towards me, I turned the good side of the machine to face him. Conference completed, I set off down the road, and was quickly parked in the workshops of Ray Cowles, the motor cycle dealer, where Cedric helped me to put things right. With my head down, I saw the Chief Inspector drive by on his way back towards Abergavenny. Another close call.

In readiness for our move from Abergavenny to a new purpose built Headquarters at Croesyceiliog, Sergeant Len Reynolds was appointed as Motor Cycle Sergeant. We had not previously had a sergeant of our own, and we looked forward to being a specific section with someone to look after us.

No, Terry Jayne had got it wrong, Mike Curr didn't get the job, and neither did I. At that time there were five of us on the bikes, in order of seniority – myself, Bryan, Keri, Dick and Mike Gunter, and there were only five bikes. So Len needed one of his own. He quickly got in touch with R.J. Ware and Sons at Newport and put an order in, unfortunately County Supplies, who usually put such things out to tender hadn't been informed and when they did, Alex Thoms the other big dealer was awarded the contract. No matter, come the day, because yes the bike had arrived at Wares, it was transferred from one dealer to the other – all being satisfied, with Len's reputation intact.

It is quite difficult to stand up and write in a pocket book without having support for your arm. It takes much practice to perfect. I was getting plenty. One day I was at Tredegar when I spotted a car go by with a car tax out of date by just a few days. The car stopped just below the clock and I pulled up, put my machine on the stand, and spoke to the driver. It was Mr. Archie Lush, later Sir Archie, who was Michael Foot's agent, as he had been for Aneurin Bevan before. He was a man well known for his good deeds in the community, and clearly the elapsed tax disc was an oversight. He explained this in no uncertain terms. The problem was he wouldn't stop whilst I put him in my 'naughty book'. It was he who helped me to perfect my system of writing, whilst walking, skipping, and running, as in the 'naughty book' he was surely going.

I once reported a motorist on Raglan By-pass for no tax, it being out of date by about two weeks, when the annual rate of duty was £15. The driver, a tidy chap of moderate means appeared in the Magistrates' Court in front of Major Bull, and was fined the exorbitant sum of £25. I felt absolutely gutted for the chap myself, so God only knows what he felt. Some monhs later I booked a resident of Raglan for the same offence, only on this occasion it had been out of date for months rather than days. I duly appeared at the local Courthouse where I gave my evidence, and the culprit was fined the princely sum of £1. That's justice. I never ever booked anyone for that offence in Raglan again, preferring to follow the offender into the next Court area, so that he could be punished, but in a fair manner.

There was another offence which I had difficulties with, that was the speed limit for goods vehicles on the open road, which was 40 miles per hour. The problem was that it applied the same for a Mini van as it did for an eight wheeled lorry, or it did in those days. I was booking a chap from Manchester in such a vehicle for such an offence at the bottom of the Heads of the Valleys Road one day. He produced his licence and it was clear that he was a totter – he would be disqualified on the points system for this extra offence. He was a reasonable sort of chap, showed me photographs of his five kids, and it was a firm's van, it was his livelihood. I told him to be more careful in future, and put my 'naughty book' back in my pocket. That did more good than any summons – he started crying uncontrollably, such was his relief. Goodness knows what he would have done if I'd actually booked him. He departed with the following words – "NOT ALL COPPERS ARE BASTARDS – ARE THEY?" No, not all coppers are!

Abergavenny to Croesyceiliog

William Farley, OBE, MC, QPM, DL.
Chief Constable of Monmouthshire
1964-1967.
Chief Constable of Gwent 1967-1980.
(South Wales Argus)

Having been in command of the Monmouthshire Constabulary, and latterly Gwent for seven years, 1971 was a year that our Chief Constable, William Farley must have regarded with considerable pride. That was the year that the Headquarters of the Gwent Constabulary moved from Abergavenny, where there just wasn't enough room anymore, to a new purpose built building on a green field sight adjacent to the Croesyceiliog By-pass. The facilities were excellent. The operational side of the Force was housed in the main structure, whilst there was an amenity block housing canteen facilities, accommodation for courses, lecture rooms, a gym and the like. Some short distance away across a roomy Traffic Yard were situated the Workshops. Everything was new, the most up to date equipment was installed everywhere. The Operations Room was the most modern in the country, the workshops even had a rolling road. It was excellent, and all I was told, for three quarters for a million pounds. What a bargain.

Come the day of the move, or really the days, as it was to be no mean feat, we all had to muck in. Fox the Mover, the Cwmbran based removal firm was employed to carry the majority of the things which we took with us to the new world, whilst a considerable amount of surplus and redundant equipment was left in the old. A lot of stuff had to be disposed of, and huge gangs of us were employed taking load after load of it to the Council Rubbish Tip at Llanfoist. Others went to the new building to unpack. We were all very busy. That is nearly all of us. One of my colleagues had managed to pick up a piece of paper at Croesyceiliog on the first day, and was happily roaming the building three days later, still carrying the same bit of paper. He didn't do a stroke. Fortunately he was in the minority.

Mr. Walby had retired at about the time of the move, and his place had been taken by Chief Superintendent Donald Wilding, a silver-haired man of distinguished appearance, who had had a lot to do with the specification of the new building and who had arranged the logistical side of the move. Mike Curr, who was now a patrol car driver, was seconded to the new boss, to assist with the move. He excelled at his new role.

After amalgamation, the Traffic Department had been split into two sectors, North and South, but after the move to the new headquarters this arrangement was done away with. Whilst we still had satellite Traffic Stations at Castleton, Abergavenny, and Blackwood, the majority of us were stationed at the new building. The motor cycles were all based at headquarters, with the temporary exception of Bryan Knight who stayed at Abergavenny and Doug White at Castleton. The Southern Sector motor cyclists and those from Abergavenny joined forces under the supervision of Sergeant Len Reynolds. There were plans to increase the newly formed Motor Cycle Section even further from a sergeant and nine to a sergeant and fifteen constables. This entailed acquiring an additional six motor cycles, all Triumph 650s, which we old hands took over, and gave our old ones to the sprogs. My new bike was EWO 732K. When delivered they were not fitted with farings, but after a lot of controversy these were subsequently added. I preferred a bike without a faring and so did Len. My thinking was that if you dropped a bike the faring would invariably get smashed. Whereas without, you could soon put a machine right. However, the majority had the day. It took a lot of getting used to, after eight years of wind and rain, and yes I did get to like them, as you were certainly more sheltered, and had a greater level of protection. No crow would hit you in the chest with one of those fitted.

When you had a staff appraisal from your supervisory officers, whilst they discussed your performance, your present station and welfare needs, no one actually allowed you to read what was said about you. Well I discovered where they kept these reports, and they were not locked away. Thus on one dark Sunday evening when no one was about, a colleague and I, equipped with a torch – embarked on our voyage of discovery. I wished I hadn't, and so did my mate. He was described as – 'Not likely to set the world on fire', whilst my report stated, 'might be handicapped by his boyish appearance'. I'd like to be so handicapped now.

Soon after we had moved to the new building it was arranged for the Traffic Department officers to undertake a 'Traffic Officers' Course in the brand new lecture room allocated to the department. Girlings Engineers were to lecture and give demonstrations on braking systems on the first morning. Mr. Wilding, our new Chief Superintendent, opened the course, and whilst welcoming us to the new facilities, hoped that we would look after them as if they were our own home. Woe betide anyone damaging anything. As he spoke a Girlings' engineer preparing for his lecture, poured some acetone into a plastic cup, just behind the boss. Of course it went straight through, but no matter, our careful lecturer had a metal wastepaper bin underneath to catch the corrosive chemical. Unfortunately, it managed to find its way through even that, and there was a large area of rubber flooring tiles needing replacement.

Of course the assembled students exploded with laughter – it couldn't have been better or worse timed, whichever way you look at it. My ribs ached for days.

One of the newcomers to the bikes was Constable Ian Barnard, who had built up an enviable reputation for himself as a rugby player. He was a really big sort, who was nicknamed 'Barney'. He suggested that now that we were a proper Motor Cycle Section we ought to have a tie of our own made. Everyone thought it was a great idea, but what should the design be. I suggested a rat on a motor bike, everyone loved the idea. Bob Morgan of the Driving School, who had an artistic flair was commissioned to design it, and it looked quite effective. So much so that I sent off an order for twenty-five to a major London manufacturer who advertised in the Police Review. It wasn't long before the powers that be got to hear about it, and Uncle Len and I were summoned upstairs to see the boss. No, we hadn't asked permission, and we couldn't have one. What would the press make of it if they got hold of it. 'A rat on a motor bike', definitely not. I cancelled the order. But they still turned up. Whenever we wore them, which at first was pretty rare, it was usually with a scarf. But no, the press never did get hold of the story. I've still got mine.

The concept of 'Intensive Policing' was born and buried during this period. The idea was to swamp an area where there was a specific problem usually associated with road safety with a number of Police motor cyclists. The very presence of this more than usual number of officers would have the effect of calming the motorists down, traffic would flow at a reduced speed, and the accident rate would be reduced. Lives would be saved. The area chosen in April, 1972 to launch 'Intensive Policing' was the main Western Valley Road, the A467 Newport to Brynmawr Road, but covering from Highcross to Blaina and Nantyglo. It entailed for a whole month four of our number patrolling either for three hours in the morning or three in the evening at the rush hour. Yes it worked. There wasn't a single accident in the month on that stretch of road. If there was a problem, it was that the same motorist could be booked four times by four different officers on his single journey down the valley. The South Wales Argus certainly got hold of that story – it made the front page. Whilst a smaller version was tried on the A449 Raglan to Caerleon Road, the concept didn't last long.

When Mr. Wilding had briefed us on the original idea, we were asked if we had anything which we would like considered. I remember that one of the boys suggested that we ought to have cardboard motor cyclists situated along the road. I quickly chirped – "Why do we need cardboard ones whilst we've got wooden .... like you". Everyone broke out into laughter, the originator of the idea and the boss too. We used to have a time of it.

Always mischief making, the motor cyclists, needed watching if you wanted to escape unscathed. Once one of them put a Dyno-tape message 'I am a sludge gulper' across the top of anothers crash helmet. That wasn't a problem, it was the fact that it took him two weeks to discover it, and when he stopped a driver, he couldn't understand why they were laughing.

Len Reynolds was a good sort. A crowd of fifteen young riders was no

Gwent Police Motor Cycle Section at Police Headquarters, Croesyceiliog in 1973.
Back row (left): P.C.s Malcolm Thomas, Bob Miller, Mike Gunter, Jeff Adams, Geraint Davies, Doug White, Mark Griffiths.
Front row: P.C.s Chris Walters, Ian Barnard, Bob Turner, Sgt. Len Reynolds, P.C.s Bryan Knight, Idris Davies, Paul Heaton, Mike Samuel.
(Absent: P.C. Dick Jones).

(South Wales Argus)

easy task to supervise, but he managed it. He was lucky as well, because he had a good hard working crew. A record of the number of persons reported, accidents dealt with, checks made etc., was kept. It was aptly called the 'Rat Race'. It didn't take long for someone to discover its whereabouts, and any officer having a quiet time of it, was soon able to catch up by giving himself a few extra ticks.

I once booked another officer, and having suffered an enforced stay in Coventry, it meant a great deal to me when Bob Hitchings, who was now on the Driving School, walked up to me in front of many others, grabbed my hand, shook it, and practically shouted "Well done". Thank you Bob – I won't forget.

Ian Barnard had a Heavy Goods Vehicle Driving Licence. I remember we had escorted an abnormal load to Trefil Quarry, and Barney had to have a go reversing this 70ft long outfit, the tractor unit of which was a Yankee 'Mack'. He did very well, and only had to go forward once or twice. The driver asked me if I wanted a go. Being unfamiliar in such a vehicle he stayed in the cab. Under his directions the outfit went backwards without a single shunt. When we stopped Barney asked "Was he showing you?" No, I did that all on my own – didn't I?

In 1972 I attended my fourth motor cycle course at Bridgend, it being my second Advanced Refresher. This time I was with two South Wales men, one from Neath, the other from Cardiff. Surprisingly Barney was on his Standard course – a mere sprogg. Again I managed to get a Class 1 with a Final Ride mark of 87. And still I was only 27 years of age, but now I could put a bike on the stand – I was all of twelve stone. I had never been the fastest motor cyclist around, I didn't have the nerve for that, but I did have a reputation for riding within my capabilities, and as we know, my accident record showed a clean slate – didn't it? They did trust me to come back at the end of the day – at least.

The improvements in the road network in Gwent had been considerable in the period I had been a motor cyclist. We had a dual carriageway all the way from the County Boundary at Monmouth to the M4 Motorway at the Coldra. In the oil crisis of the early 1970s the speed limit for hitherto unrestricted roads was reduced to 50 miles per hour in order to conserve fuel stocks in the country. I was on a Triumph 750cc bike at the Yat one morning when I saw a large saloon passing south bound. I followed, the lights were green at Monmouth for both of us, and it took until about three miles south of Usk before I managed to get to him. His speed had been in excess of 110 miles per hour for the duration. I know because for that considerable distance I had been doing that for most of the way, and never getting to him for the first twenty miles. I was getting too old for that sort of thing. The bike was one of a new batch delivered and allocated to the next generation of riders. Like those that had gone before it vibrated like a road drill. When you stopped after such a long high speed journey, your guts were upside down.

I was at Headquarters one evening when a Chief Superintendent approached me, stating that a relative of mine was asking about me. Apparently on that evening there was a Special Constables Quiz in the

Amenity Block, and all manner of dignitaries had attended. I was from a Lancastrian family, so I couldn't possibly have any relative in the building, there just weren't any in Wales apart from my immediate loved ones. The Chief Superintendent went on – he's the Chairman of the Police Authority, and he'd like to see you. This was music to my ears, I replied honestly with more than a touch of flippancy – "I've always wanted a relative on the Police Authority". Anyway I had to go and meet him, and the gentleman concerned turned out to be Mr. Tom Warkley, who was the first Chairman of the Police Authority in Gwent, a kindly man who I had not met before. We had a short conversation, as a result of which when I went home I related excitedly this to my wife. "Yes, that's Uncle Tom". What could anyone say.

A great part of a motor cyclists duties was to attend Chepstow Races and other events in the summer months like agricultural shows, fetes and the like, in order to assist in keeping the traffic flowing freely. Many people preferred to park their vehicles on the roadside, verges, gateways, entrances and the like, having little or no consideration of others. But these duties carried out, it was always pleasurable to enjoy the atmosphere at shows, and to get someone to put a flutter on for you at the races. Invariably you were provided with a meal, and only on one occasion did I ever find a wasp on my plate, still sporting its yellow stripes, but minus its wings.

On one particularly foul day, the wall of the motor cycle garage was blown over by the wind, landing on top of the parked bikes. Someone had seen a rider come in and park, yes it was Bob Turner, and fearing the worst everyone set to with a will to clear the debris to rescue our mate. After about ten minutes of concentrated effort we could see he wasn't there – no surprise, so urgent had been our mission that nobody had notice that Bob was actually helping us.

Early in April, 1974 Mike Curr was promoted to the rank of sergeant. Terry Jayne was right, he got there before me (not on the bikes though). I was glad for him – not bad with nine years service, but I was disappointed, I was ambitious too, and I, like anyone who has been qualified for four or five years, wanted to improve my standard of living and that of my family. The pay was still woefully poor. Many had left the service for that single reason. I had stayed, hoping to see better times. Anyway I had faced triumph and disaster before. Nothing for it – show good grace, congratulate him. I kept my tears for home.

Not many weeks later I was called in off patrol to see my boss Mr. Wilding, who told me to be outside the Deputy Chief Constable's office at 10am. It was a Monday morning – could it be? When I went upstairs, there were twelve of us, four sergeants and eight constables. The Chief Constable, Mr. Farley was away, and I found that the other eleven had been told on the Friday to report on the Monday, whereas I was told on the morning. No one said I was going to be promoted. I sat there for an hour or two whilst all eleven entered that room, and each had exited excitedly. When my turn came, I was convinced I was there for another, perhaps more sinister reason. But no, I was promoted. Mr. Woodcock said so. It was April 19, and ten days later I was to start at Newport Central as a Patrol Sergeant.

Lightning Strikes Newport

Having been a motor cyclist for nine years, and only having had twelve months experience of beat work, if that – it came as no real surprise to me that there was an awful lot I had to learn. Fortunately my new Inspector Keith Harris, realised this, and set about equipping me for my new role as a Patrol Sergeant at Newport Central, at what was and still is the busiest Sub-Division of the Gwent Constabulary. Our shift, 'B' Relief had three sergeants, Sid Games in the Charge Office and Ron Lewis and me outside. Sid was a seasoned campaigner who you couldn't fail to like, particularly with that disarming smile of his, and Ron was an ex-C.I.D. man who had held the rank for about a year longer than me. It was quickly decided that I would take charge of the foot men on the Town Centre and Pill beats, whilst Ron had the outskirts – Malpas, Castleton, Rogerstone and Bettws, together with the paper work. It was a sensible course – Keith Harris being no fool.

The busiest shift was afternoons, where the job went at a hundred miles an hour from the minute you walked through the door until you finished. Whereas, at least on mornings and nights you had a short quieter spell at the start or finish of the shift. Most of the men were probationers – with under two years service, a good many having much less, and required a lot of support. However there were a few senior men outside such as, George Luckett and Lyn Force. Keith Harris believed in giving the men maximum support, and thats what they got.

Whilst I had long standing experience of dealing with traffic related matters and had dealt with crime, I was lacking in technique as regards interrogation and crime interviews. I soon identified that there was a young natural on the shift. That was a former lorry driver from Chepstow, Dave Edwards, and hardly a day went by without him having someone locked up. If I had just sat in on his interviews he would have thought I was checking up on him, so there was only one thing for it, I came clean. And that is how the sergeant with almost eleven years in got his lessons off a probationer with only as many months. He was good, very good, and as a result of swallowing my pride I too became good.

Having got on my learning curve, I had to address the new sergeant syndrome. One day I was a constable and the next a sergeant. Apart from the odd incident, I soon convinced the shift that my tail was not for wagging, and we all got on pretty well. A good tight knit unit, all working and going in the same direction. I was lucky, I had been brought up with a father who had the philosophy of 'you never back anyone into a corner which they cannot get out of, and you never let anyone back you into a corner that you cannot get out of'. Sound sense. A principle I always had in mind when dealing with others. I had a principle of my own, however – 'would I want this man with me on the beaches of Normandy'. If the answer was yes, fine, but on occasions I admit I would have preferred to have been at Dunkirk with one or two.

With so many probationers, there was a manpower problem, as these men were required to attend all manner of training courses. Whilst in theory you had about twenty men outside, with training needs, leave, sickness, attachments, court commitments and all manner of duty abstractions, you were sometimes lucky if you were running the area with five men outside. That with some of the most valuable and vulnerable commercial property in the force area, and definitely the biggest windows. Yes glass does break, and you needed men to ensure it didn't. Also the Westgate Square – looking up Bridge Street and then Stow Hill resembled something more like Las Vegas at one or two in the morning, when the clubs were turning out. Alcohol, is something that makes me want to sleep, but unfortunately with many it has a far different effect. The early hours of the morning, even in the week, let alone the weekend, often resembled Custers Last Stand, with large groups hell bent on trouble. Hardly a night went by without at least one fracas, and a number of running battles was more like the norm. But alas, Custer didn't have to contend with women, and they can be more violent than men – believe me.

I once had to attend on top of a nightclub where a man was threatening to jump. I have always had a fear of heights, and even writing this my feet and palms are beginning to sweat. There was only one thing for it – I explained my plight to the potential suicide victim, who fortunately took sympathy on me, and came down. Good chap.

When patrolling down through the town it was customary to see each man on each specific beat as you went. You might see one in High Street, and then the next south of the Westgate Square at the top of Commercial Street. It was a comfortable way of doing things, because everyone knew where you were. That was never the way I worked. I might see one man for a conference at the Westgate, and the next at the Dock Gates at Pill. It kept me fit, and I was soon known as 'Lightning', as no one knew where I would strike next.

After eight months I was feeling some confidence, I had managed to rectify my shortcomings. However, it was not to stay the same, as I was told I had to transfer to 'A' Relief where I was to be the only sergeant outside. Yes after eight months, I was to have the only one of the four shifts to not have two outside patrol sergeants. Well I was a loner on the bikes. It might work. Now 'A' Relief had two long serving constables, indeed they had the longest service in the Division – Dill Rogers and Jack Williams. Dill was the senior man in Pill, and was the driver, and had two younger walkers, whilst Jack was the Town Centre Driver. Both had considerable experience, oozed with common sense, and were definitely the type you needed with you at Normandy. There was only one thing for it, I invented a new rank of corporal, and whatever anyone thought, it worked, and worked well. You couldn't have two more loyal officers. Indeed whilst Dill was in Pill and I was going through from the Town, Jack looked after the paperwork, and particularly at night was mobile whilst I walked.

These were the days when economy was the order of the day. The 'Panda' cars, of which there were five, four on patrol and one for supervision, together with the big van, an Austin, were restricted in the mileage they could do. I think the petrol allocation per vehicle went down to two gallons per 24 hours.

You could do a lot with that couldn't you? When an officer said he was down to the red, I quickly learnt to ask, was that top, middle or bottom red? It's surprising what you can get from a Ford Escort when the gauge is on red.

Another complaint from the drivers was the condition of the cars, and one evening I inspected the whole lot. I did have a certificate in my pocket signed by the Chief Constable stating that I was authorised to examine motor vehicles in accordance with the Road Traffic Act and the Construction and Use Regulations. Suffice it to say, the Sub-Division saved an awful lot of petrol, as four Escorts were put off the road immediately as being unroadworthy. The outskirts van and the dog handlers van just passed my inspection – and they were the only two vehicles used at Central for the next few days. The big van was already at Headquarters receiving attention at the time, and its return a few days later coincided with an irate telephone call from Headquarters, it was back up there within twenty minutes. One of my senior officers was more than a little upset about my actions. He even threatened me, and in front of witnesses. One thing was sure the vehicles at Central were never allowed to get in such a poor state again, and it wasn't long before they were replaced. If I was to be rewarded, it was clear it wouldn't be in this world. I certainly made no friends in high places.

A call went out one night that there were intruders in the Cold Store in Shaftsbury Street. This was an imposing looking building with steel mesh type doors at the front. The problem was there was an eighteen inch gap at the top, and someone had seen two burglars entering over the top. On arrival a few of us shinned up and over via the same route, whilst others surrounded the building outside and waited for the key-holder. Torch in hand we searched the building, walking past huge sides of beef and the like. Imagine our surprise when we found two such carcasses, one with leather jacket and the other with blue woollen jumper. How they thought they would not be seen, goodness only knows.

We had a good shift, with good men. They worked harder than I did when I was a constable. Two of the shift subsequently transferred to West Mercia and did well for themselves – John Scott and Chris Knight, whilst Jeff Davies went to C.I.D. and Chris Brown became an Inspector with quite a short service.

When you identified a young probationer who was having difficulties, it was important to get someone to take him under his wing, or take him out yourself, to see if you could help. On one such occasion I had walked for about ten minutes, and was explaining to the young chap, that he had to be more inquisitive, when from the bottom of Hill Street I saw someone walk up to a car in the distance, open the door, close it, then walk off. I said to the bewildered officer, "What was he doing?" Anyway we walked up to the person, and enquired what he was doing. He explained that he had put a parcel in his car. Could we see? It turned out to be a carrier bag full of joints of meat and steaks. Where did he get it? Oh, my mate. Well it transpired that the mate was a cook in a large hotel in the town and the management were very interested. One for theft and one for handling. The young constable soon had the idea, and yes, he did come good.

I once dealt with an accident involving a Police Officer on an afternoon shift. He had turned in front of a motor cyclist, and was subsequently prosecuted. Months later I saw the middle aged rider, who had received twenty-two separate fractures down the right hand side of his body, hobbling around the street after a very long period in hospital. And it meant a lot to be thanked for the manner I had dealt with him.

My worst night was when the shift was down to four out. There were three drivers and one walker on the town. The foot man had found a break at a premises in Upper Dock Street, and it took some time to call a key-holder and to arrange to board up the premises. Whilst this was going on someone screwed every shop in one of the arcades, all eight or nine of them. I spent the next hour or two like a commissioner at the entrance, meeting the shop-owners and accompanying them to their shops. They deserved better – but what could you do with such a staff shortage?

I was once accompanied on an afternoon shift by an officer from a Government Department, who had been seconded to the Division for a week to get a feel of what Police work was all about. Well he certainly got that. I saw to that. A bomb report at South Dock turned out to be a bag of chicken bones, another in Austin Friars, a suitcase, full of clothes. He was surprised that I opened them. The town would never move if I hadn't. It was a question of judgement, you had to use it. Another visit was a domestic in full swing, oil spread, the waters calmed, and onto a shoplifter. This was a shoplifter with a difference. Two women had walked around a supermarket together, loading their trolleys with identical items at identical prices. One paid at the check-out , the other stayed looking around waiting for the till receipt to be brought to her. The store had tumbled it. She was arrested. A visit to her home, revealed three children, all identically dressed. It was clear that her kids were wearing and feeding on the proceeds of other expeditions. Wasn't I going to do something about this – No way, she'll be done for what the shop caught her with. A woman alone, three kids – take further action and they wouldn't even have been wearing socks.

Our shift comprised men who were married with up to three children. The pay was still very poor for probationers particularly. Some were even able to claim D.S.S. supplements of one kind or another. At that time we were working a forty-hour week. Which meant that on continental shifts, working twenty days out of twenty eight. Seven on – two off, seven on – two off, seven on – three off, with an additional day off taken within the cycle. Some shifts allowed the men to take this floating day when they liked. On 'A' Relief we had none of it. Inspector Edgar Shephard and Owen Pugh the Charge Office Sergeant and myself had difficulties enough in running a shift which was so often short. I allocated every man his day on a roster basis, so that following the long weekend off, finishing with the Sunday, three or four men were allocated a day off on each day for the following Monday to Saturday. Come the day, if we were short they worked it and were paid overtime, of which there was precious little about. It worked well it gave us a little extra cover, and if they did take it off they had it in the week where they should have had it. The superintendent quickly worked out my game. He addressed the shift – "Wouldn't you prefer to take your extra day when you

58

want to"? Yes they would. How the hell could they afford to take a duck in pay. I don't know – but they did.

Alas in 1976 Dill Rogers and Jack Williams decided to retire. We had a quiet drink after their last shift, because they finished on the same day together, in the Ship and Pilot in Pill, and had a more formal do in the Con Club a week or two later. My God how they were missed. Unfortunately Dill didn't live to enjoy much of his retirement – it was the saddest of funerals. I thank them for their friendship.

Creatures of the Night

I had been very happy with my lot in the Police Service. True the pay wasn't that good, but I'd enjoyed being a motor cyclist for nine years and I had spent two hectic but equally enjoyable years as a Patrol Sergeant at Newport. However, I was astute enough to recognise a storm cloud as the next. It was the practice for one of the patrol sergeants to spend a period of around six months as the sergeant in charge of the Plain Clothes Section. This had accounted for the shortfall of sergeants and why I had been on 'A' Relief on my own outside. I was aware that Colin Kenvyn's period on the section was due to end, and thinking that I might be next, I endeavoured to get as good a deal as I possibly could for myself. I spoke to the Divisional Commander, Chief Superintendent Robert Catstree, and no sooner had I opened my mouth, than I was deemed better than any pressed man. The job was mine – no arguments. I have often thought about my habit of talking myself into things and yes, I really have tried to rectify it. But here I was, with no way back. The only concession that I was allowed was I could choose who I had with me to work.

The Plain Clothes Section at Newport was made up of a sergeant, and a constable who had service in the job, in other words a mature man. The section dealt with prostitution, gross indecency, pornography and the like, and was more commonly known within the job as the 'Vice Squad'. It usually entailed a period of six months on such duties, as to stay longer was thought to expose officers to the risk of being corrupted. Or so I understood the Home Office view was. Anyway my interview with Mr Catstree was progressing, and he tried to assist me in the direction of choosing a colleague. He suggested, helpfully, a number of men, and each time I came up with what I regarded as valid reasons for turning them down. Robert Catstree was not a man to waste time, and he concluded the interview by giving me a copy of the Divisional Strength Sheet, and stated that I was to be back in the morning with the name, as I was going on the section, and there was no negotiating. Well that was quite clear. I've got the job, but I can choose my partner, and I've got until the morrow to do so.

The very nature of this job dictated that I needed someone who would be completely loyal. Someone I would be able to trust. Someone who would be my man. It definitely had to be an officer who I would want with me at Normandy. There was such a man in Central. I had made it my business to spend time in the Collator's Office, and Gordon Britton, a Constable with more service than me, a Borough man, had been most helpful. He had impressed me with his knowledge, and I had always liked his style. I didn't tell him. I didn't want him to have time to find the reasons for refusing. But I had decided that he was my man.

The next day I was back in the Chief Super's office, and the name was given. Gordon Britton was on duty downstairs, and he was quickly

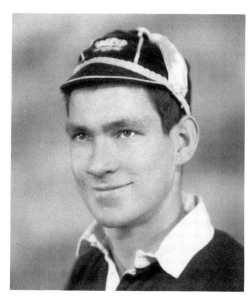

Gordon Britton, Welsh International Rugby Cap. He and the Author were stationed on the Vice Squad at Newport together.

summoned. He came in, he was asked what he thought about it, and in true Gordon Britton style said – yes. We went out, having been given our starting date, and thereafter planned our strategy. Clearly this was an evening job, and knowing that we only had six months, or so we thought, we decided that a shift pattern on these lines would be best. We actually worked nine 6p.m. - 2a.m. evenings to one day shift, and by the time we had finished had become true 'Creatures of the Night'.

On our very first day, we started early both arriving just after 5p.m. Gordon had been an electrician before joining the job, and when anything went wrong with the electrics it was a case of 'call for Gordon, he'll know how to fix it'. No sooner had we started, sitting down in our dingey little office next to the Control Room to familiarise ourselves with the paperwork, than the call went out for 'Gordon'. Apparently the electrics were faulty in the Police Club down below, and Gordon would soon sort it out, or so they thought. This was our first day, I had plans, and my partner spending hours on the electrical circuits of the Civic Centre wasn't one of them. Gordon tried to fix whatever was wrong, but in the end the whole building was without electricity, and those who are paid to fix such things were soon called. I got Gordon back, but we didn't have any candles, so we had to venture out into our brave new world.

In preparation for this new job, I had bought a green jacket, brown trousers, and a pair of brown brogues. Just the job, never get noticed in these. And after all we were to be paid plain clothes allowance, and a car allowance to boot, as yes we had to use our own. On that first evening we made our first pounce. We arrested a man for importuning for immoral purposes in a public toilet in the town. He had entered the toilet so many times that the only other explanation would have meant that he was in desperate need of a catheter or a

61

colostomy bag, and he was talking to others as well. Either that or he was a painter and decorator and kept running out of paint every two minutes, and had to discuss with all and sundry the new decor. But no, none of these, and the place hadn't been painted for decades. At that time I was 31 years of age, but what happened next added years to me. Arrested, he wasn't coming with us. He was a big man, a very very big chap, and all the two of us could do was keep him. With great difficulty we held him. Every time we got him to the floor, to stop him running away, he got up and tried again. So whilst he made no headway in making good his escape, we made none in getting him towards a vehicle to take him to the station. This went on for ages, and at last someone had called the Police, and Colin Kenvyn, now a fortunate man, a patrol sergeant, which I wished I was back doing, arrived with a few men to assist. Thank you men. My new gear, brand new too, was ruined, the brogues were badly scuffed, my trousers torn, and the sleeve of the jacket was slightly longer than it was a little while ago. Things had to get better.

I never felt comfortable with this part of the job, and whilst every person arrested for gross indecency appeared in the figures as a detected crime, so what. It wasn't so much that it was dealing with people who had a liking for playing with each other I disliked so much, that had to be discouraged. It was the fact that so many of them had wives and families, yes hard to believe, but true. It was those I felt for, the innocent families. As a result we did all in our power to get them cautioned so as not to ruin other lives. In that way the experience of being caught was hopefully enough, and they wouldn't come again. But no, some did. Couldn't they take telling?

Newport didn't actually have that big a prostitution problem. There was a relatively small number of females in regular attendance on the streets. The law dictates that a woman caught soliciting should not be prosecuted on the first occasion, nor the second, and they had to be officially cautioned twice before proceedings taken on the third occasion. Sensibly, the law allows a woman two chances to change her ways before her reputation is forever tarnished. We found women soliciting, and soon discovered their individual areas. Some would do it in the open at the back of a building standing up, and even carried an umbrella should it rain. Others would go off with the client for a short drive and return around twenty minutes later to the same spot to be dropped off, looking for another. Few took the man back to base. But a few did.

We discovered a girl who looked around eighteen or nineteen, who appeared to be being 'looked after' by a much older man. We discovered that he had a previous conviction for allowing premises to be used as a brothel. For it to be a brothel there had to be two or more females. Anyway, we found this girl in the company of this chap, and watched them for an evening. She would walk off in front, and he sidled along some distance behind. It didn't work so they went for a drink. On coming out of the pub, we knew where they were heading back to. As a result, it being dark by now, we parked the car, in a position opposite where he lived and opened the windows wide, turned our radio off and waited, of course lying flat in the car. Sure enough here they come. She set up shop on the pavement opposite, and he would go behind the door. She walked out towards passing cars, and if they stopped had a conversation. No takers. When a bloke walked by she would speak to him, and at last someone bit. We could hear the conversation. By this time her minder who was in the shadows was doing the talking. The young bloke who wanted to get to know her, would have to go and get more money, he didn't have enough. So off he went, and sure enough after a while back he came. The conversation started again, and the deal was struck. But by this time Gordon Britton and I had sprung into action. Gordon called for assistance, and I half crawled, half ran across the street, putting my foot in the doorway, so that the older chap would not be able to claim no knowledge. He was there, she was there and so was the prospective client. Subsequently at Crown Court he was convicted of allowing premises to be used for prostitution, there only being one female and sent down for three months. The girl was only sixteen, and she said her minder had not taken any money off her, so he was acquitted on the immoral earnings charge.

On another occasion we saw a girl operating alone, was she eighteen? We did not know. Anyway, she approached pedestrians – men, and walked to the kerb when cars passed. Eventually she was picked up. Gordon and I decided to wait, follow, and see what the score was. They drove towards the coast road but they didn't stop. They turned and drove to a nearby valley town. They got out and went in the house, the upstairs lights went on. Thirty or was it forty minutes later they came out, jumped in the car and set course back towards Newport. It was dark now. The car stopped at the traffic lights by George Street. We jumped out. I spoke to the driver, a man in his thirties. Gordon spoke to the girl. She said it was her uncle. Funny. They were arrested and taken to the Central Police Station, where he admitted having sexual intercourse with the girl, he had paid her, the notes had been wrapped around his card so that she could contact him in the future. Tragically the girl was only 14. She looked much older. Parents and Social Services were called. She was examined by a doctor, she was a virgin. How could this be, the chap had said he had had sex. What had apparently happened is that she was a clever little minx for one so young. She must have crossed her legs in a certain way, and he thought he had penetrated. I know it takes some believing – but the doctor, Dr Hymen Shepherd, had taken swabs, which after examination at Forensic, had come back positive – yes there was sperm externally, and wait for it, there had been sperm internally – the doctor stated that it travels. So there we are. But what to do? She would have to be dealt with by Social Services. But what of him? The girl had denied it all. No prosecution ever took place, who would have been the witness? It all happened to Gordon and me.

On another occasion we saw a girl that we had cautioned once, come out of her house, she went into a shop, came out with a bottle of milk in one hand and a bottle of 'Camp' coffee in the other. She looked at a passing car, it stopped, she got in, and before you could say 'Jack Robinson' they were parked out on the Coast Road, the coffee and milk not being required. And they didn't have a kettle anyway. So here she was – both cautions spent. Be a good girl – it's not worth it. The next time it's for real. I was pleased that she stopped. That made it worth while.

Another girl, who was already convicted, yes a 'common prostitute', was caught three times. She wore a different wig every time – blonde, brunette and auburn. She was caught a week later in Cardiff and dealt with there for all the cases.

Part of our duties entailed vetting the strippers, no, not in private. Some of Newport's nightclubs had strip shows on certain evenings and one even had a show at lunchtime. It was our job, yes at Police expense including a pint or two of beer, to sit and ensure these ladies did not offend public decency. We needn't have worried, as seeing a sagging ballerina prancing around a stage as if she had a club foot, or a worn out cart horse with cholic, they tended to look worse the more they took off. Grace, there was a fat lot – it was as well that the lights were turned down. I duly reported – 'indecency no, positively obscene'.

We once carried out an investigation into a 'Contact Magazine'. You know, one which advertises certain unmentionable services. Men advertised at cost, women for free as to do otherwise would have risked a charge of immoral earnings. I had the names and addresses of those who had advertised, and interviewed most, but as delicately as possible. I even found a couple not many doors from my home advertising for something called swopping. No thanks.

If there was a problem working with Gordon, it was that he had been a Welsh Rugby International – yes, another one. He was more well known than even he would have imagined. We were carrying out observations one night, real incognito stuff – when two chaps passed the car. One said, you see that chap in there, that's Gordon Britton, he played for Wales. A mixture of broken cover and hero worship.

When we started an evening shift, whilst I carried on with the paperwork, Gordon went up into the Collators' Office to see what was happening. He had a wonderful memory, and always remembered a face. One night, having seen a photograph of someone who was forever hiring cars with no intention of returning them, and knowing that he had a Hillman Avenger out, Gordon actually picked him out as he passed in a Hillman Hunter, and he had never seen the chap before. On another night, and again not strictly Vice, but we were forever helping our divisional friends, he picked out someone he'd had for burglary years before, the chap was with another. We followed them from outside the Cameo Club in Commercial Road, all the way through the town, where they disappeared by the Cambrian Road Car Park. We stayed there for half an hour, thinking they were screwing a building society office, and to our surprise turned up looking like Father Christmas. They had done the Parcels Office on the Railway Station. We waited for them to unwrap some of the packets – make sure they hadn't just found them as it were, and pounced. Hard to believe they even pinched an empty packet with a Policeman's handwriting on, the contents having been taken on an earlier occasion. The one went down for twelve months for that job.

At the end of our six months, and having been helped by a number of men from the Support Group at various times, our period of six months was extended for a further three. And so it went on.

Towards the end of my stint on Plain Clothes, Edgar Shepherd who was now the 'C' Relief Inspector retired, and no decision having been made as to his replacement, I spent a few weeks as Temporary Inspector on his shift. Edgar was as sound as a pound. He had been the Federation Branch Board Secretary years before, and had been on the Joint Central Committee, a high office to hold. Owen Pugh retired soon after. Owen was magic, and I always remember those great card schools we had down at the Police Club after our last afternoon shift. When Olive the stewardess threw us out we continued until the small hours in an unoccupied office. For very small stakes of course. No one won a fortune and no one lost one either. Those were the days. When I had been on 'A' Relief on my own outside, Owen had been a power of support. He made it all possible.

At the end of our nine months, of which Gordon had run the show for two or three weeks with John Drinkwater helping, we returned to a more normal lifestyle. I went back to 'A' Relief, and he to 'B' Relief, but I was always pleased that after a very short period he was promoted. With Gordon I had reached the fields beyond the Normandy Beaches.

P.C. Glen Jones who served with the Author on the Beat at Newport and on the Motor Cycle Section.

Motor Bikes Again

Having returned to 'A' Relief at Central, Paul Murphy was the Station Sergeant, whilst the boss was Kendrew Davies. Jeff Rodway arrived soon after from Bramshill, and with two outside sergeants he had the town and I had the paperwork and the outskirts. Newport was as busy as ever.

One night Glen Jones had discovered a man who had been stabbed in the rear end at the approaches to the railway station. He was oozing blood, and needed hospitalisation urgently. I arrived before the ambulance, and Glen pointed towards the station and stated that the culprits had gone that way. He wanted to follow, but he was covered in this chap's blood, and was coping well, so I ran over the station bridge to the centre platforms, just in time to stop a train departing with our villains. Help soon arrived and they were taken to the Civic Centre, and the actual culprit identified. On another occasion I had gone to Glen's assistance in the John Frost Square where he had arrested someone, and had had to crouch with prisoner underneath him, in order to beat back an angry and hostile crowd who were hell bent on doing him injury. I will never forget the feeling of pride I had on seeing him holding on for grim death, staff in hand. As a result of this about eight others were apprehended. The problem was that Glen needed treatment for his injuries. So guess who had to sort it out?

The three years at Newport had seen a slowly maturing patrol strength. And with this growing maturity had come a feeling of self confidence in the men themselves.

However, there were a few newcomers to the shift. One night, one was giving a breathalyser to a motorist at the Westgate Square. The problem was he had left the driver in the vehicle whilst he was standing outside, and the keys were in the vehicle. The young inexperienced officer had just identified a positive test, when the traffic lights changed to green, the car sprung forward and was away. Not even its number having been taken. What shall I do Sarge? Forget it, you'll never find it now. That was down to experience, but he would never make that mistake again, and for that matter all that arrived on the shift would be the wiser for it.

The month after I left Headquarters to go to Newport, Mr Woodcock had transferred to Devon and Cornwall as Deputy Chief Constable, it being a much bigger force. Mr Palastanga had taken up the reins as our Deputy and the post of Assistant Chief Constable had been filled by William Rostron from Sussex, who had originally served in Pembrokeshire. One sunny May morning in 1977 I was sent for. I arrived outside Mr Rostron's office to be met by Chief Superintendent Mike Keohane who was now the head of the Traffic Department. I was ushered in, but already had an inkling of what was coming. There was a vacancy for a Motor Cycle Sergeant. I was quite happy on the street at Newport, and having found that I could live without the constant athlete's foot, and skin complaints caused by the bike engines, I was

The first B.M.W. 750cc motor cycles delivered to Gwent Police in September, 1974 with Sgt. Len Reynolds and P.C. Bryan Knight.

(South Wales Argus)

Gwent Police Motor Cycle Section at Police Headquarters, Croesyceiliog in September, 1978.
Back row (left): P.C.s Andrew Lamb, Mike Gunter, Ray Neachell, Chief Superintendent, Mike Keohane, Assistant Chief Constable William Rostron, Chief Inspector Mike Frost, P.C.s Ian Champion, Lyndon Wallace, Chris Szwajcer.
Front row: Glenn Jones, Jeff Adams, Glyn Bailey, Sgt. Paul Heaton, P.C.s Phil Evans, Ian Barnard, Dean Smith, Bernard Williams.

Advanced Motor Cycle Refresher Course at Bridgend in May, 1980. The Author riding on loose surfaces. *(Western Mail & Echo)*

69

The Author on B.M.W. 750cc motor cycle, index no. OAX 25 OR.

(Gwent Constabulary)

in no hurry to come back. It was put in such a way that I should be jumping at the chance. Not me, I know that if an Assistant Chief Constable calls you in, and offers you a particular job, you take it. But jump, no. If I had jumped I would have been over a barrel. I had always served where told. I know I managed to get back to the bikes a couple of times, but on this occasion I was going because the A.C.C. wanted me to. Not because I wanted to. Therefore Len and I swapped places, he to Newport – and he liked it, and me back on the bikes.

I wasn't very excited about my move. I had been qualified for promotion for a number of years, and if I was to fly I would have to make it to the rank of Inspector soon. It was not to be, not for a long time.

Gone were some good friends; in the intervening three years seven of the old team had departed for pastures new. Geraint Davies to National Welsh, Stumpy (Chris) Walters – the nearest we had to a stunt rider, Dick Jones to Cwmbran and Bob Turner to the same division. Doug White, Idris Davies and Mark Griffiths had gone on the cars, but Mark eventually transferred to Devon and Cornwall. Bryan Knight was still there, as were Malcolm Thomas who was originally of Mid-Wales extraction, Barney who had acquired the nickname 'Super Ted', Mike Samuel who I once, years later, saw hit three sixes and three fours off the same over. Bob Miller who had made his name removing a fence post with his leg on the Treharbour Road, Mike Gunter the most immaculately turned out of us all and cool handed Jeff Adams, were all still riding bikes.

Newcomers during my absence accounted for Glyn Bailey on a revisit, having been on the bikes before; Andrew Lamb and Ray Neachell who liked to make a bike sit up and talk, Bernard Williams whose twin was in the job on C.I.D., Ian Champion, Dean Smith and Lyndon Wallace made up the rest. Seven gone, seven arrived.

Very soon after Mr Keohane suggested that I ought to visit other forces to see how they operated, in order to maximise the effectiveness of the section. I was also to align more closely the riders with individual shifts, so that when I was not on duty they had a feeling of belonging at shift level as well as at section level. I visited Sussex on my own, but Dean Smith came with me to Surrey where they had a motor cycle formation team – we might be on Come Dancing yet, some unkindly said. Gwent had a very active group of motor cyclists, and whilst I duly reported my findings, all twelve or was it sixteen pages of it – we had done it all before, six years earlier in fact as far as 'Intensive Policing' was concerned. I was asked if there was one single improvement that I could adopt, and I plumped for the NATO type sweaters. We wore tunics under our Barbour and Belstaff jackets, and they never looked very good, almost always creased, and were most uncomfortable. Thus we were each issued with two sweaters, 100% wool, and my weren't they smart. The boys loved them. When making the recommendation I omitted to say that whilst they were wearing them in Sussex they had paid for their own. I never got tumbled, but those in Sussex couldn't believe it. Ah well, if you don't try.

Wide Loads continued to make up a large part of the working day, but

Motor Cycle Section Open Day, 1978.
Sgt. Paul Heaton, P.C.s Mike Gunter, Jeff Adams, Bernard Williams.

(South Wales Argus)

whereas fourteen years earlier, we had to fight our way through the traffic from the front, now, with improved roads and much motorway and dual carriageway, it was a far more leisurely affair, following from behind. Much more civilised, but had the disadvantage that you were for ever clearing your mouth of dust and grit, and your lungs were for ever full of diesel fumes and smoke.

The three years away had seen the disappearance of the old B.S.A. and Triumph machines. There had been six Norton 750s, but only one remained – and I was threatening to put that on the rolling road to get it up to a respectable mileage, so that we could get shot of it. No, Len had done a good job. We had sixteen BMW 750cc bikes – SAX 601 and 602N, JDF 500 – 504N, LDG 99P, and OAX 243 – 250R. Yes, one had got bent and was replaced by SWO 227S. I couldn't believe it, here was a machine that you could ride at speed, sustained high speed if required, and unlike anything I had ever ridden before – you got off feeling as fresh as when you started. The things actually forgave you too – if you went into a bend too fast you could switch it off and still come out the other end. Whereas a British bike had to be thrashed around a bend or you came off, and when you reached journey's end you felt as if you had something akin to Parkinsons Disease, such had been the level of vibration. Yes, Len had done very, very well. We were lucky.

Now we were expected to cover all manner of functions, Royal visits, Race and Point to Point meetings, and shows. We barely had time for patrol. Another area we were used on was Newport County football matches, where we tried to keep the roads clear, escorted opposing supporters to and from the grounds, and during the match itself were able to supplement the inside men. Football crowds are similar to thoroughbred racehorses. If you don't expect trouble you don't get it, but it is sensible to be prepared. If you expect them to play up – they sure as hell won't let you down. The next few years were to have at least a fortnightly ordeal during the season. I hated it – soccer was not my game.

On one occasion a group of motor cyclists and beat men were escorting a crowd of, at that time, well behaved Swansea City supporters from the railway station to the ground via Corporation Road. Things erupted when they fell in with a crowd of home supporters, fighting, screaming – how were decent local people to cope? The one with the biggest mouth, stopped for breath near the George Street traffic lights. So inattentive had he been, that the next thing a Corporation double decker had stopped unfortunately on his foot with the back wheels. It only took a few seconds, and I was too far away to intervene, before the lights changed to green. The youth had been silent with the wheel on his foot, but all you saw then was a screaming Roger Bannister departing alone on the horizon.

I attended at the match between Newport and Exeter City one year. I never felt happy about it, yes a feeling of real unease. So disturbed was I that my four men were ordered to stay by the gates under pain of punishment of a tall hat and cape. I still don't know what happened that day, but a sergeant on duty was subsequently stripped of his stripes. I don't know the facts, so I

Heavy Goods Vehicle Road Check at the Magor Intersection of the M4 Motorway, 1980.

Briefing at Newport Central Police Station in 1977 for an evening operation regarding Stolen Motor Vehicles.
Seated at table (from left): P.C.s Lyndon Wallace, Bernard Williams, Dean Smith, Chris Szwajcer, Jeff Suffield (Dog Handler), John Alford (Motor Patrol Driver), Sgt. Paul Heaton. *(South Wales Argus)*

cannot comment. But I had had dealings with that man in the preceding years, and my opinion of him was as a loyal, honest, hardworking sort that you could set your clock by. A man you would have needed at Normandy. On the other hand the Superintendent who was running around in the crowd like a chicken with no head, would probably have got me drowned before I reached the beaches. I'm sure that God does know what happened, as only the sergeant lives today. I salute his courage.

On another occasion I was sent to Andover where BMW were handing over to another force the thousandth machine to be delivered to the British Police. It was interesting, as I had been here before when Norton road tested all their machines on the Thruxton Racing Track. At that time we were only allowed one circuit, and it is difficult to get the feel of a racing track until you know where it goes, there being no hedges or guide to the course. But here I was again, with the full range of BMW machines and cars to try out. I kept to the bikes, as in the cars BMW had a man to cool you down. But what an experience, I'm glad I was still young enough to enjoy it.

Oh yes, I had in the old days visited the BSA factory at Armoury Road, Birmingham. What a tragedy that the British motor cycle industry died. But I'm told that it's coming back and they aren't like they used to be – they don't rattle!

Gradually older members of the section departed for pastures new – Bryan, Barney, Mike Sam, Glyn, Mike Gunter, Jeff, Bernie and Henry to the cars, Malcolm to the Met and Andy to Ebbw Vale. They were replaced by a new generation of motor cyclist – Chris Szwajcer, Phil Evans, Glen Jones, Jeff Howells, Gary Morgan, Dai Tanner, Alan Dunn, Bob Morgan, Pete Fou'weather, Greville Phillips, Sarky Jones, John Brown, and Mike Jones.

In 1980 Mansel Thompson, who was in charge of the Road Safety Department and the Driving School put my name forward to attend an Advanced Refresher Motor Cycle Course at the South Wales Police Driving School at Bridgend. It had been eight years since I had attended, and I had no wish to put myself through the ordeal again. Anyway I was 35 now, surely that was too old? No amount of wriggling could get me off the hook, and in the end Superintendent Peter Rowlands pointed out that the men on the bikes would expect it – and I was going. Inwardly my fear was that having held a Class 1 ticket for over twelve years I might come back with a Second, if I came back, that is.

On arrival at Bridgend I noted that my original instructor, Dai Evans of over fifteen years ago was running things, and whilst he didn't instruct me, he undertook the Progress and Final Ride Assessments. I knew Dai, but I also knew that if I wasn't up to it he'd be the first to tell Gwent. Strange to see, but I hadn't seen Norman Abrahams since I had put two marks on him on my Standard Course all those years ago. There were to be two students, both sergeants, such a course had never been run before, and the South Wales Echo even did a feature on us – which luck would have it, I never saw. Come the first day out on the open road, Norman led the way, with our instructor behind, and a struggling Paul Heaton in the rear, trying to keep up. Norman went like a bat out of hell, and I had thoughts of being put to shame. I thought long and hard about this on that first night over a pint of shandy. Think man, you know the score – come to Bridgend knowing it all and you're in trouble. Come to Bridgend with some idea, and improve as the fortnight progresses and you might survive and you might even keep your Class 1, albeit with a probable 86. So that was my plan.

On one progress run we went to Devizes, and Norman led from Lydney towards Chippenham. When we stopped at the appointed place to change over, I had fallen back a bit, and when I pulled up Norman had even lit his pipe. "What kept you?" he said. Right – we'll see. So I led from there to Devizes. I planned my revenge, and saw my chance as we were leaving Chippenham. As the D-restriction signs were looming up ahead, I overtook the single car in front, putting one between us, before we reached the open road. I kept the throttle open all the way to Devizes, didn't wait at all. And when Norman, Dai and the instructor pulled up, I was half way down a Hamlet, lying on the verge. Dai didn't say a word, but I had seen that twinkle in his eyes before. Very little of the course was in Gwent's area, and it was particularly nice, following a ride to Oxford, to be told to lead from the Severn Bridge to the Coldra via the A48 Chepstow Road. Oh how I went, and yes Dai and I waited a few minutes for the others to arrive.

On the final day, Norman and I tossed for who should go on the Final Ride first, he won, and departed down the drive. After about forty minutes and five or six cigarettes, I saw them return. They went into the garage for about ten minutes. I waited, and eventually we were off. It went really well. When I could go, I went, where there was a problem I held back, but always in a position to go when the opportunity allowed. Another thing was helping me, I was getting to know these roads in and around Bridgend, so my chances of getting caught were reduced. The ride completed, we had coffee, and waited to be told the result. I couldn't believe it I had 89, the highest I ever had, and once again I put two marks on Norman. I admit it, I would have happily settled for an 86. But 89!

The problem with this, was when I returned to Gwent, everyone wanted to show me that although I had 89, they could ride better than me. That's not what it's all about. The mark also reflects a safe ride, and a person always likely to arrive. Whereas if there is the slightest doubt about your ability to get there, consistently, safely, you don't get the mark at Bridgend. Some of my boys were itching to show me. I once came back from Abergavenny, a road I knew very well, in double quick time, only to be overtaken at the bottom of Pentwyn Pitch on the approach to the dual carriageway by a jubilant officer who had hammered through the danger zone, junction being left and right, with cars waiting. My next trial was at Monmouth towards the Yat. Yes I chose my ground well. Always picking an area where I had greater experience of the road than my men, who were raring to have a go. The RAF were moving Buccaneer aircraft by road at night to St. Athans, and three of us were awaiting the arrival of such a load, and were parked at Dixton, Monmouth, when the call came through that the load was coming towards us from Ross-on-Wye. I started my machine, rode around the roundabout, and held it through each gear for the maximum revs. up Layston

Bends (no bends there now, but it still holds the name). The other two followed, Dean Smith and Lyndon Wallace. We came over the top like rockets, down the straight towards the bend with the Truckers Cafe on the left half way round. It was a case of in for a penny in for a pound. I had to give it a go. The Truckers was well placed, as Wally failed to take the bend, and used the forecourt as a de-acceleration lane. No harm done. But Dean was still there. I came into the Yat flat out, holding on to the last moment to brake and slow for the slip road, and then onto the bridge. A smart little slow down signal, and Dean was in the back of me. I stopped he clouted the back of me. No damage, both upright. But they didn't take me apart did they? Dai wouldn't have given me an 89 if he thought I was going to get up to that sort of nonsense, so that was positively the last time.

The next time a high speed was called for, I was travelling towards a call at St. Arvans where potholers were trapped. Barney was with me. I let him go, and didn't see him after the Coldra until I arrived a minute or two behind him at the site. That's better, use your head.

Mr Keohane decided that we needed to have an Open Day, yes A Motor Cycle Section Open Day where the public were invited to meet their Police on Motor Bikes. Frank Smith, a natural organiser, put it all together, and what an excellent job he did. Inspector Frank Smith had a way of getting the very best out of these events, and the kids loved him, such was his way. We had motor cycling competitions, ice-cream, fire engines, ambulances, old vintage cars, all manner of displays on speed and breathalyser equipment, and even a tour of the Operations Room. Such was its success, that in all subsequent years it was extended to become the 'Open Day' for the whole force.

The Chief Constable suggested a Good Driving Campaign, where the best drivers received a suitably engraved Biro pen. These were carried in our pockets, and if we saw a good driver, someone showing common sense, courtesy, or a particularly fine piece of driving, we stopped them, congratulated them, and made the presentation then and there. As everyone knows, ladies are amongst the most courteous of drivers, and this was reflected in the numbers awarded to their sex, it had nothing to do with their age, or anything else. But yes, blondes did seem to figure heavily in the numbers. I recall stopping a National Coach Driver and making the award. At this time the vehicle was in a lay-by, and I will never forget seeing the driver walking up the aisle of his vehicle showing the pen to all his passengers with such obvious pride. Yes, Mr Over it was an excellent idea.

In 1980 Mr Farley had retired after sixteen years in command of the Gwent, and former Monmouthshire Constabularies. It seemed strange that a man who had held the office for so long was leaving. We were so used to him, seeing him, and knowing his likes and dislikes that it was difficult to comprehend a new Chief. But in that year John Edwin Over, was appointed Chief Constable. He had been a Metropolitan officer originally, and had served in Surrey and latterly in Dorset as Deputy Chief Constable, but with a period of Secondment in Hong Kong. He was a big imposing fine figure of a man. He looked every inch a Chief Constable. You never mistook it. His whole bearing, speech and temperament was that of a leader. Yes, things

"I don't think he wants the damn pen!"

GREN Cartoon depicting the Gwent Police Good Driving Campaign.

(GREN/South Wales Echo)

were changing. Whenever a Force has a change at the top, or even in the top three, there is always going to be change. Change is good. New ideas. He wouldn't be a Chief Constable if he didn't put his own mark on the force. I didn't always like what he said, but I have always, believe it or not, liked strong management. And here was a strong manager.

We had been operating Breathalyser Campaigns for a number of years. In Gwent you have one of the highest possible chances of being caught, of anywhere in the country, if of course you drink and drive. Whilst the instructions varied every year, the accent was on saving lives. And I am sure that the way the officers of the Gwent Constabulary carried out their duties – giving of their best, helped achieve this. Gwent had a reputation in this regard. If you drove an unroadworthy lorry over from Ireland, you didn't risk it through Gwent, not if you had any sense. Overweight lorries were quickly identified and dealt with. Once a 32 tons gross outfit was detected with 21 tons over its permitted gross vehicle weight, you would wonder how it could have moved. Road Checks were held with the Trading Standards Department of Gwent County Council, the Department of Transport Vehicle and Traffic Examiners, the Customs and Excise and other departments, and the results were disturbing, given the number of prosecutions which followed. One small incident stands out in my mind. Primarily because the officer with me won't ever let me forget it. We stopped a French lorry which was put off the road for some offence, and the owners in France had to be contacted to arrange to remedy the problem before it could proceed. Well as you know I left school at fifteen, and whilst I had picked up a smattering of Spanish and Portuguese, I was the one who spoke to the man in France. Like a fool I started the conversation with "Hello Senor". Dean Smith was doubled up. Now can you stop telling the tale, please?

There had been a major problem with stolen vehicles at Newport – can one ever remember a time when there wasn't? As a result an operation was mounted comprising local beat and C.I.D. men, Support Group and Traffic patrol cars and motor cyclists. The results were most encouraging. It did however mean that most of the motor cyclists had to work evenings. One night during the campaign we were called to assist at a public house in Pill, where there had been a disturbance, and the landlord was having trouble ejecting some of his customers. With about fifty or more people now out on the street, trouble erupted, and I made an arrest. Whilst I was attempting to put the chap in a police van I was set on by four women, and between the five of them I took a fair old hammering before assistance came. The peak of my crash helmet was broken, and I received an injury to my chest. The job done, I continued to have aches and pains for a few days, and in the end had to seek medical attention. I had received cracked ribs, and as the doctor said, it won't get better until you have a period laid up. Yes Police Officers do not generally welcome sick leave, as they realise that colleagues are left with a greater work load – they like to do their share, and not let the side down.

Whilst that is generally true, I did once manage to detect a pattern of sickness with a group of my riders working the same block. Every time a long weekend of mornings was worked one or other, but only one, would ring in sick on the Sunday morning. I soon realised whose turn it was on the next occasion, and wished him – the day before – a speedy recovery. That soon stopped that nonsense.

I duly reported for duty on the evening of December 31, 1981 to be told that Mr Bill Rostron, the Deputy Chief Constable wanted to see me. I marched up to his office. He was not a man you kept waiting, a keen disciplinarian. As I made my way upstairs I wondered what I was going to hear. What had I done wrong? What had one or more of my flock been up to? Where was I going? And in the next chapter we find out.

First with the News

It was too early in the evening for Bill Rostron to want to ring in the New year with me, and anyhow I was needed on the 'Breathalyser Campaign' in which I had always had a big involvement. I was met outside the office by Superintendent Rowlands and on entering was invited to sit down. This was usually a good sign, if you were for the high jump you never sat down. I was told that I was to be the first Public Relations Officer in the force. This was the new dawn in the Police Service, and Mr Over wanted to promote the image of complete openness. In fact the new job was to entail liaising with the Press and Television and to ensure that all that happened in the Gwent Constabulary, the good – of which there was much; the bad – yes we made mistakes and to admit to them was to have credibility; and the indifferent – to ensure that there was none, were objectively portrayed. This was going to be no small job. It entailed working directly to the Deputy Chief Constable, and would bring me into contact with the Chief Constable on many occasions. If the Press wanted to know something, and I did not have the answer, everyone in the force was to assist in finding it. Yes, openness was the key word.

I was to complete my last shift as the sergeant in charge of the Motor Cycle Section that very night, and was to start on my new role on the day after tomorrow, i.e. January 2, 1982. This was exciting stuff. No one had ever done this in Gwent before, and it was a big thing to be invited, no told that I was to set it all up. Len Reynolds was to take over on the bikes, I was pleased, as that was his first love, and the men would be all right. Better Len than some whizz kid.

I later met the Chief Constable to discuss the post. Mr Over told me that where interviews were to be carried out with the media, he wanted the man at grass roots level, the man actually dealing with the incident to see the press. Whilst it was openness we were about, this was to give the public that feeling of confidence they deserved, and which was our – the Police Service's – duty to provide. It was not a question of just promoting the Gwent Constabulary, but to promote the area as a whole. Gwent was the word, Gwent and the people who live there. If there was a murder I was to take the pressure off the investigating officers, and to keep the press and television informed. In that way those who dealt with such tragedies could get on with the job of investigation, only stopping for interviews which were to be arranged by me.

I absolutely loved the job, and the Press liked it too. They now had a point at which they could converge with all their questions. If they wanted to do a feature on some particular aspect of Police work Paul Heaton made it possible.

I was sent to South Wales at Bridgend and Avon & Somerset in Bristol to see how they set about things. I was impressed, and did learn a lot, but in those areas they had a whole department or were part of one, whereas in Gwent I was to be alone. I saw Mr Rostron on my return, who was most interested in what I had learnt. I stated that we would have to do it differently, but he let me get on with it. It was like being a motor cyclist all those years ago, my instinct as a loner held me in good stead. A loner who was to project the team image. Yes we in Gwent, above all else, were always a team.

Right from the word go, I had things to say. We had been hit by blizzards in Gwent, and the rest of the country really. Police officers were rescuing the sick and the elderly, men were walking thirty and forty miles round trip to work, young probationers were delivering babies. Many acts of selflessness had been carried out, and the constabulary had done some fine work to try and keep things running. I had kept the press up to date, and was like most, walking to work each day, albeit only three miles each way.

Bill Rostron called me to his office. What had I done on the snow and our involvement? Get down to *The Argus,* there are the facts. I was given the whole file. How will I get there? You'll find a way, use your initiative. There was very little traffic moving in the county. I donned my winter clothing, Wellingtons and all, and went down to the Traffic Department to try and scrounge a lift. I had to be joking. I had my instructions, the Argus were expecting me, so off I set on foot. If it took till nightfall I'd rather go in the direction of the Argus than in the direction of the Deputy. And yes I was disappointed, a department that I had championed for so long was prepared to let me freeze. However, someone was to look after me that day, because after a mile struggling on foot, an off duty officer running his wife to work came across me. He was one of very few to venture out, and had difficulties in driving, but he took pity on me – well he had been on my shift years before, and I'd treated him kindly as a probationer. You reap what you sow. After pushing and shoving, and much use of shovels, I was lucky enough to arrive at Maesglas outside the offices of the *South Wales Argus,* Gwent's own evening newspaper. I went inside where I met Meryl Rees who was in charge of reporting Police matters. She was absolutely amazed to see me, how had I got there, had I walked? I just smiled bravely – I didn't want to spoil it. Well yes, the snow and the Gwent Constabulary's involvement in it made a wonderful feature. The morning was almost gone, I set out again, on foot. I felt that the eyes of all in *The Argus* were upon me, some with near admiration, others with a more honest view – look at that fool! I decided that a walk to the Central Police Station in Newport would provide a suitable refuge for lunch. And yes I did walk all the way. Lunch taken, pleasantly chatting to old friends, and on with my gear again and off back to Headquarters in the snow. By this time Western Welsh were operating a short service from Newport to Cwmbran and not knowing this, was pleasantly surprised when a kindly bus driver peeped me on Malpas Road. Thus part of my journey was to be in comfort. Arriving at the traffic lights near Burtons' Biscuit factory at Llantarnam, I alighted, thinking that the short walk up the hill wouldn't do me too much harm. But no, I was in luck. Noel Williams, a friend, of Pontypool R.F.C. fame stopped, and I rode in style back to Headquarters, sensibly getting out of his car out of sight of the building. I walked in, people thinking that I had walked all day. No, like Mr Rostron had said, I had used my initiative. But no, I never did explain to him that I hadn't walked. An ambitious man needs all the points he can get.

After the big thaw, and on the morning of the Chief Superintendent's Conference at Headquarters, the press and television turned up to cover the presentation of 'Commendation Certificates' to those who had done the most worthy deeds. I say most worthy, guardedly, as everyone had done a good job during the blizzards. Television crews, reporters from all the local newspapers, including the dailies, *Argus, Echo, Western Mail,* and BBC and local radio. All turned up for this big day. I was on the crest of a wave, and following the interviews and photographs, even Mr Wilding who was the Chief Superintendent in charge of the Administration of the Force, held out an orange juice for me. Yes Paul Heaton – that was your day. No one could believe the coverage that I had achieved, let alone me. But by now I had friends in the press, radio and television. I had built up a rapport. I had made it my policy – 'nothing was too much trouble', and they appreciated it.

When the two probationers that were stationed at Newport Central had

John Over QPM, CPM, DL, Chief Constable of Gwent 1980-1993
(Western Mail & Echo)

failed to get to work that eventful day and reported for duty at their local Police Station – Caldicot, no-one could have foreseen the consequences. Called to a lady's home, they delivered her first child – never flinching from their duty. They also helped to give birth to my credibility as a Press Officer in the Gwent Constabulary. I had magnificent coverage of this. First the announcement that they had acted as midwives, secondly their award of Commendations by the Chief Constable, thirdly the announcement that they were to be the child's Godparents, and finally national coverage on the main news on both channels at the church. What a story, and what a pair of tidy boys they were. I was able to show one of them my thanks in the future.

There had been a scare concerning a deadly disease which I think came from pigs, or something. Anyway it had received national coverage in the press, and coincided with the theft of some valuable equipment from a Ministry of Agriculture laboratory. I was told, I hope in good faith, that there was a risk to the felons, and duly arranged wide coverage – TV, radio and press. Sure enough once the culprits heard this they practically ran into the Police Station to confess. But what of the follow-up story, were they all right, what had the doctors said? No follow up, so I might have been set up – it's important to keep your credibility with the press, lose it and you'll never get it back. I still smiled about it though. Dai Jones you're a cunning devil.

I learnt something from this incident, as a few weeks later a burglary had occurred at a school in the valleys. The culprit or culprits had made themselves coffee – the cheeky beggars, and instead of using powdered milk, had without knowing it used ground glass. Apparently there was no actual danger, or little danger, and when running the story only the facts were given. But yes it worked a treat. I had learnt from Dai before. Thanks.

Although my duties were in relation mostly to press liaison, I was always called the Public Relations Officer. This was good. At that time there was a newly formed Complaints and Discipline Department in the force. When an irate member of the public rang in to complain, they often asked for the Public Relations Department, and in consequence I got calls that were not really meant for me. However, we all know how irritating it is to be passed around on a telephone switchboard, so I always had a sympathetic ear, and many who rang were actually trying to get it off their chest as it were. On one occasion a lady complained that the Policeman walked into her house with her son without knocking. Yes the Bobby was with the son. No big deal you might think, but when you realise that the lady had her nightie on, it takes on a whole new significance. But she thanked me, and was satisfied that I would speak to the officer. I did. I always did pass on to the various officers the grievances felt by members of the public. I recorded the details in writing, but at one stage I was dealing with more complaints in Gwent than the Department actually set up for the purpose. If the person wanted to take the matter further I would transfer the call. But in six months I never got caught – if I had I would have had them on my back – they'd have given me one of those funny forms.

I was able to use my own judgement in this job, and whilst it all went very well for most of the time on occasions I made the odd error of judgement.

When I did I got it in the neck good and proper from the Chief or his Deputy. But pound for pound I was winning.

The local papers ran a series 'Know Your Local Bobby' and this was fine, but on occasions the papers would save the little articles I had written up and produce a couple of weeks together which appeared to be more like 'Know Your Local Force'. The Police Federation Joint Branch Board had been generous in their praise, and had told Mr Over so. Alas they soon changed their minds, such was the level of my output.

Mr Over had been very wise in appointing an officer to undertake liaison with the media, because it certainly had an effect. The public were better informed, and good honest stories were appearing about us. Whilst he rarely was featured in interviews, preferring to see the man on the ground giving the story, when he did he came over really well.

The mark of a true professional came to the fore one day. I had been asked to arrange an interview with him by a students' magazine or the like, and when I waited in the outer room of the Chief Constable's office for them to arrive, looked out of the window. I was horrified to see walking up the drive, yes the main drive, two youths with bright orange hair or was it bright red? Their hair was done up like a Mohican Indian, greased up into a comb, with the sides shaved. Get out of this one Heaton, I thought. They even had a photographer and a real reporter with them. I needn't have worried, Mr Over didn't bat an eyelid, gave a very sensible interview without even the hint of embarrassment, and our budding reporters went away having enjoyed tea and biscuits, in clear admiration for my leader. It ranks as one of 'the' experiences of a lifetime. I just hoped I wouldn't enjoy another like it.

I did enjoy this job, it only lasted for six months before I moved on, but to have been the first was terrific.

Tragedy – Scene of fatal road accident at Pontyrdryn in July, 1982.

(South Wales Argus)

Tragedy

I had held the rank of sergeant for eight years, and had enjoyed every minute of it. The pay had improved considerably following the Edmund Davies enquiry, and the Police Service was well worth being a member of. A good job with good pay. However, I had been qualified for promotion to Inspector for some time, and whilst I had been on a number of Promotion Boards in front of the Chief Constable, I had never really clicked. I had always tried to be what I thought those interviewing me wanted me to be. Sounds Dutch now I know, but that's how I had always approached it. Come the day of my interview with the Chief Constable, his Assistant Mr Clarke, and the Detective Chief Superintendent Gordon Jones, I had gained considerable confidence in my own ability, born in part from my past dealing with the press, which immodestly, I excelled at. When asked to give an account of myself, I stated the errors of my past boards, and that I wanted to show them who and what I really was. For the first time I was myself. The board went really well, and whilst there was little feedback, I didn't need any, I knew it went well.

Shortly afterwards I was informed that I was to be appointed as Temporary Inspector on the Traffic Department on motor patrol, with the 'A' Relief. By now the head of the department was Chief Superintendent Roy Ellis, and what a personality he had (and still has). His deputy was Superintendent Peter Rowlands, with whom I had served on a number of occasions. The shift had two sergeants – John Evans and John Fitzpatrick, both experienced men, and a group of constables the like of which was rare to see. They were good. But I had always known that.

One of the first things I recall was attending a fatal road accident on the A449 dual carriageway just south of Usk. A saloon car had crossed the central reservation and struck an articulated lorry travelling North. Tragically the three occupants of the car had been killed, husband, wife and their child. It was clear that a rear tyre on the car was deflated and forensic examination revealed that the tyre which was steel braced had a slight exposure to the elements causing a corrosive effect in the wall. At speed the tyre had failed. I never ever repaired a tyre after that. Remember, if it's punctured – throw it away. So efficient were the shift, and so thoughtful for the feelings of the relatives, that I might as well have done a sponsored walk to Monmouth and back. The job would have been done well enough without me. But there were occasions when I was to be more than needed.

* ***Author's Note:*** *I have deliberately set out not to deal with fatal road accidents in this book – but in the one case there is an important warning, and in the other the sheer magnitude of the incident makes it necessary to give some details. I have, however, kept descriptions to a minimum, and dealt with the operational information only.*

In July, 1982 I dealt with a Police vehicle road accident on the Treharbour

A Double Decker bus had collided with a Low Bridge with the tragic loss of six lives.

(*South Wales Argus*)

Road, some way from Croesyceiliog, and on the morrow was en route with Sergeant John Evans to re-examine the scene. As we drove up The Highway at Croesyceiliog, the call came over our radio – 'Road Accident Pontyrdryn, casualties, possible fatal.' So instead of turning right for Treharbour Road, we turned left and drove via Chapel Lane and were soon at the scene. It was a scene of utter devastation. A National Welsh double decker omnibus travelling from the direction of Avondale Road towards Pontnewydd had collided with the Railway Bridge. The bridge, being rather low, was only suitable for single deckers to pass under. A double decker could not pass this way. The top of the bus, the complete roof had been sliced off and was lying on the road to the rear of the vehicle. Two officers from Cwmbran had arrived first and had set in motion the initial actions in what was clearly a major incident. Ambulances and fire engines together with other Police Officers were soon on the scene. I quickly assessed the situation and could see from my visit to the upper deck that many were injured and some had been killed.

I quickly set up a radio control, using Policewoman Pauline Walters, a smart efficient young lady as the operator. She was to log calls in and out to record details of all arrivals and departures of personnel, and she was magnificent. Bryan Knight, her partner, was at the scene, and Bryan knew without speaking that he was to be the officer in the case. With his experience and four by two how could it be any one else? The road was closed off, using a traffic crew at one end and local officers at the other. The nature of the incident was to make it important that passers-by did not come that way, and all were asked to go back away from the scene. The public were marvellous and assisted in every way possible. The press and television, because yes, they soon arrived, were politely asked to wait for a short period. And bless them they kept back until told it was clear, without a murmur of objection. I asked Headquarters to arrange with Newport to set in motion a casualty bureau at the hospital, and also to duplicate this at Croesyceiliog, so that all calls went through to Headquarters, but the actual information was collated in the first instance at the Royal Gwent Hospital. We had all trained for this before, yes the Police, Fire Service, Ambulance Service and the Hospital. But this time, unfortunately it was the real thing.

By this time Temporary Chief Inspector Bob Smith had arrived with Sergeant John Fitzpatrick. My two sergeants arranged for the measurements to be taken, photographs etc., and helped supervise the scene. Rescue of the survivors continued, and Ambulance, Fire and Police personnel assisted. By this time I saw two very experienced Detective Constables from Cwmbran who were anxious to assist. I had three of the most experienced men at my disposal. I spoke to Bryn Knight and the two detectives, Laurie Ledley and Terry Tomlinson, and asked them to deal with the scene of carnage on top of the bus. They jumped to it straight away. Identification was to be the key word.

The Assistant Chief Constable Mr Clarke arrived as did a number of Senior Officers. I answered their questions, but they could see that we were getting on with the job. Eventually all at the scene completed, the Press were allowed through, and they photographed and filmed what they needed. They wanted to interview someone from the Police Service, and the senior officers suggested it should be me, so newly out of the Press Office as it were. I gave the interviews, it was a tragic case.

The bus had actually been on a day excursion to Porthcawl, and at that moment had fourteen passengers, of which six had died. In working out how many passengers should have been on the bus, yes it had to be confirmed, but it was found that twenty-seven tickets had been issued. Anxiety was soon overcome when the bus company stated that the fare was over £2 for an adult, and the machine having a maximum issue figure of £2 would have called for the issue of two tickets per adult. Therefore thirteen adults and one child ($13^1/2$) twenty-seven tickets.

I kept in touch with all parts of the incident, visiting the bureau at the hospital, the Casualty Bureau at Headquarters, and the officers at the scene and headquarters. The Department of Transport would have to examine the vehicle and the Railway Authorities would have to check the bridge for safety.

In the hospital a team of Newport C.I.D. men took over, and did a magnificent job dealing with loved ones and arranging identifications where appropriate. Such was the level of co-operation between the Police officers, that I went out of my way to thank them, or to speak to their senior officers, to relay the thanks of all concerned.

Subsequently the two beat officers first on the scene, the two Detective Constables and Bryan Knight the only Traffic man, were commended by the Chief Constable. Yes, our department could say thank you to others for their help, and that was in the manner of the recommendations made to the Chief Constable. However, all had thrown themselves into carrying out their duties without any hesitation. It was a sad episode. but in sympathising with the relatives, the injured, we spared a thought for the poor driver – he needed everyone's compassion. He being such a nice chap.

One thing about this which has never come out, and if it happened to me, it must have happened to others. That was the fact that I couldn't sleep that first night, nor the second. In fact on the third day I was due to go away on holiday, and decided to travel overnight. On arrival, with great support from my family, I just simply collapsed, and slept and slept, so absolutely worn out was I. These days there is a thing called 'Trauma' Counselling.

A Fading Memory –
A Time to Reflect

As with any memory the stage at which your recollections appear varies. I thought I had covered just about everything, that was until I spoke to Bryan Knight. Bryan remembered a number of interesting points.

Such as the time when I booked a lorry driver employed by Conway Dairies of Merthyr. His load of crates of milk spilt all over the road at the entrance to Hardwick Roundabout – when he was summoned before Abergavenny Magistrates and his solicitor asked him on oath – "What was the first thing the Police Officer said to you?" Came back the honest reply, "Hang on a bit, I'll go fetch my cat." Fortunately the Magistrates saw the funny side.

Bryan and I had escorted a number of Army Tank Transporters – Thornycroft Mighty Antars, to Cwrt-yr-Gollen Camp, just outside our area at Glangrwney. I had counted twelve over Glangrwney Bridge and had accelerated towards the bridge on my return to our area, and my God there was a thirteenth. It was 12 feet 10 inches wide, the bridge was the location where the singer Dickie Valentine had died some years before. Would I survive this one, I thought. The bridge is very narrow and normally you wouldn't be able to park a tank transporter alongside any other vehicle let alone a motor cycle be able to pass one. But I knew the bridge, I knew it had a slight kink in the centre. The Army vehicle couldn't stop. If I did I'd be flattened. Only one thing for it – accelerate, and as I found the little kink, ducked my head to clear under the vehicle's mirror. A lucky escape. Bryan behind had managed to stop, but as he said, he thought I was a gonner that day.

I remember the mid-Sixties were the time when the 'Ban the Bomb' movement was born. I remember because I escorted the marchers from Caerwent to Newport on more than one occasion. The Sunday following Her Majesty Queen Elizabeth II's opening of the Severn Bridge was the signal for just about everyone in South Wales and some in the South West converging on the bridge to traverse it. It was the focal point of everyone's day out, or Sunday drive. Inspector, or was it Chief Inspector Wyer by then, had instructed me to ride back towards Newport to discover where the end of the queue was, such being the volume of traffic. When I got to Newport, and not having found the end of the line, hard to believe but true – I radioed to my boss, "Shall I go back towards Cardiff?"

My memory is starting to work again – thank you Bryan. One incident which stands out on the Police Mobile Column was the day we had an exercise. We attended a briefing, and were told that the whole column would be deployed in searching for a green Morris 1000 Traveller, such and such a number. The exercise would start at 10a.m. I had a brilliant idea. We were at Newtown, in Montgomeryshire. There was only one place that Morris 1000 would be, and that's at the Police Station. It was 9.30a.m. I staked out

Gwent Police – British police Rugby Champions in the early 1970s. Author far right.

the Police Station and sure enough, come the appointed hour it moved. It moved about 200 yards, before I pounced. The exercise over, we were being regarded as 'smart arses' and my reward for saving everyone so much work and rushing around – an extra sausage with my dinner.

I was very fond of Ma Lumley in Raglan. She was an elderly lady running a little café. She had a number of cats which were forever climbing over the tables, and these cats were extremely fond of sugar. I used to be – but I haven't taken sugar in tea or coffee since.

In the early 1970s I had been a member of the Gwent Police First Aid Team, and we had competed at the Eistedfodd and all manner of places. Roy Smallcombe, Terry Fry, Ron Day, Nai Groves and others were trained at Tredegar by Jack Seabourne, a leading member of the St. John Ambulance. Others that followed were Chris Brown and Dai Tanner. I once took a party of Cadets to Avonmouth to compete in a First Aid Competition. They were good and did well. The problem was that I made the mistake of taking them on board a ship owned by the Line that I had served with, at the Docks. They were so impressed that some were starting to consider an alternative career – and so was I. These boys –   Peter Davies, Peter Jones, Peter Fou'weather, Bob Morgan and Dai Tanner – were all to work with me in the future. Yes, I nearly forgot Jeff Dyke, he was the sixth rascal.

A little knowledge is a dangerous thing. I was asked if I would carry the box for the Force Rugby team. This entailed running on and dealing with injured players – using something called a magic sponge. I did this for a few years, and indeed Gwent were British Police Champions for two of them. We were at Stafford Sports Club celebrating a victory one evening, and were upstairs. Some clown let the fire extinguisher off at the top of the stairs, and I being the decent chap I was tried to stop it. That was when Mr Palastanga walked by. Talk your way out of that. Barney still says that's why I was promoted sergeant.

Mansel Thompson and I had worked a few shifts on the cars, and one night were called to the Cwrt Bleddyn, yes the same building, but no, not the posh place it is today. It used to be a right dive – the home of venereal disease in Gwent. Well we got there, just after local officers, and two youths had been playing up and reported. When alcohol is in, the wit is out. No good reporting them, they just went on and on being a bloody nuisance. Later that night we saw the two walking down the centre of the road, yes on the white lines. We stopped and they asked for a lift. I said jump in boys – where to? They fell asleep within seconds, Mansel telling them they were under arrest for being drunk. They snored their reply. On arrival at Pontypool they cut up rough – you just didn't cut up rough when Bill Tamplin was about. Yes Sergeant Tamplin, another Welsh Rugby International knew what to do.

In the late seventies and early eighties I had carried out, in dribs and drabs, what was in fact about twelve months duties as Temporary Inspector. In fact I had been a Bridesmaid at Central, Maindee, Traffic Patrol, and Operations Room. One of the outstanding incidents concerned a road accident at Caerwent on the A48 Chepstow Road. A red Volvo 244 DL with one occupant had been wrapped around a tree head on. The driver, a young stocky individual was trapped. The Fire Service, Ambulance and Police were in attendance. Such was the poor chaps predicament that we called a doctor, and a patrol car was used to relay plasma from Mount Pleasant Hospital, Chepstow, whilst another fetched his parents. Yes it was very, very serious. As well as the Fire Service cutting away at the car, our shift were also having a go. As you know the Volvo is a car in which you have an above average chance of survival on impact. Whilst this was so, it also had the effect, that the force of the impact had caught his feet. There was great concern that this young boy would leave his feet in the car if he was to survive. You could see the doctor's concern. Happily for this young man we had Bruce Hookham with us that night. Bruce, an experienced and mature man, knew what to do.

The car was taken apart around the boy. First the roof flew off, then all four doors, pillars, everything. We got him out, and he kept his feet. He did lose a year at college, but when he got there, he walked without crutches. His grateful parents had seen all this, they knew what had been done to save him, and they made handsome donations to Emergency Service charities. The whole shift were elated by the achievement, and he ran the risk of being adopted by them.

On another occasion I was at Maindee, when I was called to a house. The husband had turned his young wife out. Their six week old baby was still inside. Our men could get no reply to their knocks and shouts. What should we do, boss? The front door went in, no messing. The man feigned sleep. But the woman would have to live there after we had gone. I woke him, said "Sorry old chap we were concerned for your safety". His pride intact, the domestic was over. And baby was fine.

I once took over a shift for a month or two which was in revolt. They had been told that they had to book at least a certain number of offences. When I arrived I was told that the instruction still held good. I argued. But no, if you know what's good for you, you'll do what you're told – that's what was said to me. I know men, I kept my mouth tight shut. In fact at the beginning of the shift I always parted with the words "Have a nice day". My mouth shut, they worked like mad to show what they were made of – booking treble the number quoted as their target. Later, I understood that Mr Farley got to hear about it, and at a supervisors meeting, or more precisely on my way to the meeting I was waylaid, and told that the instruction had never been given. Well I had heard it, but my shift never did when I was with them.

Yes they were happy days. Do unto others as you would have them do unto you.

A Bride at Last

By the time that I had returned with my family from a week's holiday at Ilfracombe I was recovering well from the ordeal of the bus accident. I was able to sleep, and having another week off had set about painting the house. I was up a ladder, brush in hand, paint all over me, when I was called to the phone. It was Mrs. Williams, that lovely lady – the Chief Constable's Secretary. Mr. Over would like to see me. Now. Would it be alright if I came in civvies? Yes. Could it be?

Twenty minutes later, immaculately dressed in my suit, smelling of turpentine and with white paint streaks in my hair, I reported at Headquarters to the Chief Constable's Office. The conversation is private. Suffice it to say he was extremely nice, and yes I was Inspector Paul Heaton from September 1, 1982 – A Traffic Inspector. A bride at last.

I had always been a Traffic man, not for me C.I.D. or Training. I knew what the job entailed, I had received years of training towards it. Initially my Chief Superintendent had been Roy Ellis, but later David Thomas and Mark Waters were in charge. I had known Mr. Thomas since we had been constables together at Abergavenny, he had originally been like Terry Jayne, the divisional motor cyclist at Abertillery on 215 EWO. After a period on patrol, mostly teamed with Charlie Horton, he had gone in the office, and reappeared outside as a Traffic sergeant, Traffic Inspector and later in charge of the Force Support Group. He was a Traffic man through and through. Mr. Waters on the other hand came from a C.I.D. background, and had been the Support Group commander when I was on Vice in Newport, and been so helpful. Peter Rowlands was second in command of Traffic, a man who I first met when he was on C.I.D. at Cwmbran, and later Verdun Coburn another thief catcher from Cwmbran. This use of senior men with a C.I.D. background was very healthy for the department, as they had no preconceived ideas and brought new thinking with them. The Chief Inspector in the corner varied. There was much toing and froing with many in the role on temporary rank, but Roger Williams spent the longest period substantively.

Sergeants, two to a shift – John Evans, John Firzpatrick, Gene Collins, John Davey, Graham Jones, Hugh Miles, Big John Williams, Roger Sweet, and Len Reynolds still on the bikes.

The other Inspectors were Frank Smith, Keith Morris, and Roger Smith, with later Bob Hitchings, John Metcalfe, Phil Maurice, Chris Barry and Gwyn Phillips. It was still a family show, but the show had changed. There were many good officers, male and female – some who went back, like me, to a bygone era at Abergavenny.

The motorway was always the number one priority, this because divisional officers, in the main were not allowed to Police it. The motorway was the traffic mans very own. Mind, some hated working it, and it was often called 'the slab'. Whilst I was originally on 'A' Relief, I also spent periods

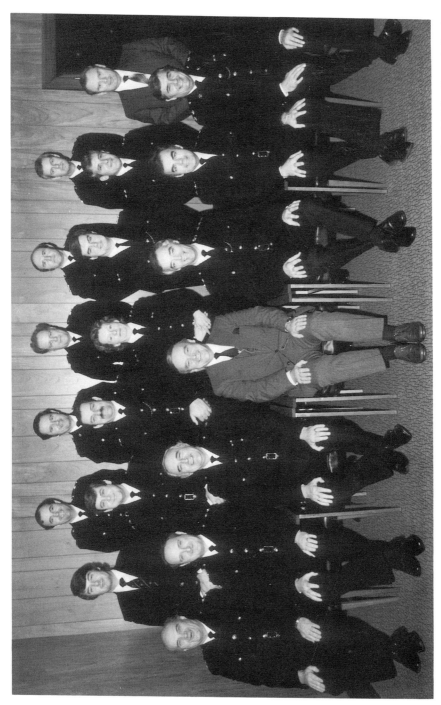

Regional Inspectors' Course at Bridgend in 1983. Author back row centre.

(South Wales Constabulary)

Her Majesty's Chief Inspector of Constabulary Sir John Woodcock, CBE, QPM, CBIM. Formerly Chief Constable of South Wales, Chief Constable of North Yorkshire, Deputy Chief Constable of Devon & Cornwall, and Deputy & Assistant Chief Constable of Gwent.

on the other shifts, and there were often periods of overlap. So I knew all the men – the good, the bad and the indifferent. Although most I'm proud to say were excellent. It was important that one knew everyone's capabilities, strengths and weaknesses, likes and dislikes, and even more important that they knew yours. Its absolutely no use having a field of thoroughbreds if they are led by a donkey. Confidence was the word, mine in theirs and theirs in mine. And I hoped that my interpretation was sound – I think so. If there was a problem, deal with it then and there. Don't leave a man to smoulder resentment for days on end. Put him out of his misery. He'll be the better for it. Anyway you've got to finish one thing before a fresh start can be made. One reason that I never made high office was that I was like an open book, everyone knew what I was thinking, because my thoughts were always transmitted into words. But everyone knew where they stood. The best way.

Life went on, dealing with incidents, road accidents, fatals, assisting divisions etc. My allocated duty in the office was Miscellaneous Property – a nightmare. Everyone had a thing about holding wheels and tyres, axles, and other bits and pieces which make up a motor vehicle. It might be needed for court. It might be. But they tried to hold onto it for ever. Gradually I got on top of this, and the room looked bare, but go away on a course, and on your return the nightmare was back waiting for you. Property was like painting the Forth Bridge, finish and start again.

During this period I attended at Bridgend for Regional Training, four weeks for an Initial Inspectors' Course and six weeks for an Inspectors' Development Course. On the initial course a student, a South Wales man had posed the question, "How do you get an officer to book five a month?" I don't know the answer in other forces, but in Gwent you'd have to tie him up for twenty-nine days out of thirty. So beware good people of Gwent – the people get the Police they deserve and the Police get the people they deserve. We are happy with you, and hope that you are happy with us. Let the politicians change it – let Gwent be amalgamated, and you'll never get us back, and all the resources that we and you have enjoyed will disappear in the direction of Cardiff or beyond.

These courses – I hated them. I am a home bird. I did enjoy the talks given by outside speakers, Dafyd Ellis Thomas, Neil Kinnock days before being elected leader of the Labour Party, and even a Tory. One gentleman stated that he never let his children have toy guns because then they wouldn't be violent when they grew up. I said that it sounded sensible, but I presumed they (his kids) didn't have a toy train set because he didn't want them to be railwaymen when they grew up. There was uproar. My end of course report reflected my comment. The one outstanding thing I noticed, indeed all the students noticed – was that every time one of us asked a question someone behind gave you a tick. Consequently, we developed something akin to verbal diarrhoea, and by the end of the course almost had a skin rash – having collected so many ticks. What utter crap

On the first course in 1983 the Chief Constable of South Wales, yes, Mr. John Woodcock, attended our end of course dinner. Mr. Woodcock, having left Gwent in May, 1974 had gone to Devon and Cornwall as Deputy and then to North Yorkshire on promotion to Chief Constable. Transferring to South Wales, a bigger force, some years later. I had always liked him, he had that ability to remember names which pleases everyone. And yes, how could he forget me, a Gwent Motor Cyclist, for so many years. He wished us well, and turning to the two Metropolitan men, hoped they would have a safe journey and pass through my area without getting stopped by the Viet Gwent. Yes we in Gwent had some reputation. A reputation which had saved lives. I wonder if Mr. Woodcock would have wanted me with him at Normandy, at least he would have remembered my name.

Shortly after this Mr. Woodcock left South Wales on his appointment as one of Her Majesty's Inspectors of Constabulary. Our paths often crossed thereafter, as when I was on the Joint Central Committee of the Federation we met at the twice yearly meetings with the H.M.I.s and at the Federation Conference. He was subsequently knighted and became Her Majesty's Chief Inspector of Constabulary, retiring in 1993. I wish him and his charming wife, Lady Woodcock well.

David East was the Chief Constable by the time of my second course, a year later. I liked him too, but rugby isn't my game either. At the end of course dinner Lord Tonypandy was the invited guest, and what an experience, what a truly nice man, and a Socialist as well.

When I was Shift Inspector on 'A' Relief a Christmas Function was arranged at the Three Horseshoes Inn at Mamhilad. At the dinner I introduced the 'Favourite Pain Award' to the member of the shift who had been the biggest pain that year. It was an extremely good natured affair. In 1987 Ian Barnard, alias Barney, alias Super Ted won the award, which consisted of a suitably inscribed framed 'Super Ted'. Runners up were Pauline Walters – a bottle of Pony, you know the drink with a big kick and Jeff Porter – a brass threepenny piece. In 1988 it was won by Huw 'Two-Heads' Miles who had a framed 'Mister Happy' and 'Mr. Glum'. The runner-up was Chris 'Jelly' Chivers and yes, his award was a framed 'Mr. Jelly'.

Gwent is on two flight corridors for civil airliners, and a considerable amount of military training is carried out by the Royal Air Force. So it was that I was sent to the Civil Aviation Authority Fire Brigade Training School at Teesside Airport to learn all about crashed aircraft. I learnt about lead lined coffins and the like – real cheerful stuff. One thing I learnt, was that survivors of air disasters are usually those who read the safety card in the pocket in front, prior to take off. Something about instincts propelling the survivor towards the exit – his subconsciousness having absorbed the directions. I hadn't flown for years, but I am an avid reader on taking my seat in a plane now.

No sooner had I got back to Gwent than I was off to R.A.F. St. Athan, to undertake an air observers course. Learning about wind speed, drift and the like. Part of the course was to enable me to navigate an aircraft. It was interesting stuff. I was extremely nervous. I remember at fourteen going up in a twin seater aircraft at R.A.F. Ternhill when I was in the Air Training Corp. Come the day, we took off in our Avro Bulldog of the University of Wales Air Squadron. Before taxi-ing to the end of the runway the pilot said "Where do you live?" He spoke to the control tower, and was cleared for take off, Pontypool bound. We were soon flying around over my house – with me pointing out to him the electricity wires and poles. What an experience. My flying suit had six pockets, and whilst we had been advised to put a sick bag in one, my instinct of being prepared for anything had ensured that I had put one in each pocket. Perhaps, I thought, if I was parachuting to earth, I wouldn't be able to reach a particular pocket, and I wouldn't want to be sick over anyone, would I?

Having flown over Pontypool, we gained height, although I understand that we never flew over 500 feet. As soon as we levelled off the Pilot stated that I was to fly us back to St. Athan. I had seen how he flew the plane this far, now it was my turn to have a go. Remember, I am absolutely terrified of

A petrified Inspector Paul Heaton about to take off in an Avro Bulldog of the University of Wales Air Squadron at RAF St. Athan.

heights, and on the journey, flight north or was it east, I had actually opened my eyes. But reluctant to look downwards. The Pilot said, "head for the motorway, then Cardiff Docks, and then Aberthaw Power Station, and then I'll take over". Well I had been in the Merchant Navy and apart from keeping the head or nose of the plane up, there was surprisingly little difference. As we neared Aberthaw the real Pilot took over. He wondered if I cared to try something different. Not knowing what he meant, I felt reasonably safe from any kind of bodily contact; I didn't think he wanted me to jump out, so with a heavy heart – a real feeling of dread, said "Yes" – why not. If he killed me he was going to kill himself, after all. We came into land, and just as the wheels were about to touch down, he pulled the lever right back and we did something like a stall and turn. Have I got it right? The plane shot back into the air turned completely head over heels like a backward somersault, and we were on the ground. Yes it was a wonderful experience, or was it? I didn't see a thing, I just felt it. Now back on the ground I felt brave enough to open my eyes again. I said a short prayer and I was out of the cockpit in double quick time.

I have rarely lost my appetite. That day was to be no exception, I had a lovely lunch, and back to the classroom for another briefing. This time we were on our way towards Brecon, and yes at the appointed time, we were actually above the Church steeple or was it a tower. Yes, right above it. My teachers had done well, and my navigation was spot on.

The R.A.F. personnel were magic, and my Police colleagues and I had enjoyed it enormously. So much so that the following year I was lucky enough to be invited back, to see what I had remembered. Whilst I will never conquer my fear of heights, I have learnt to cope with it. The important thing was to do the course – and keep my nerve. It wouldn't do for me to go back to Gwent having chickened out. No, better to endure and conquer. And better to be on the beach at Normandy than flying overhead, I thought.

A Difficult Job

The Assistant Chief Constable Mr. Clarke departed for a top job within the Police Service in London and his successor was Joe Frost, who became Deputy on Mr. Rostron's retirement. Mr. Rostron had been a strict disciplinarian, and woe betide anyone who got on the wrong side of him. However, he was in other ways a kindly man. Yes kindly, when it came to welfare matters, he would really put himself out for a worker, and for anyone who had a health problem or the like. The force had appointed a Welfare Officer, a most suitable man, Basil Bustin taking on the role. Not many people realise that Basil had been an apprentice jockey, and when he had given up, his replacement had been none other than Lester Piggott. Basil was a very approachable man, and made many peoples lives the happier for his intervention.

One year I had great difficulty in obtaining annual leave dates which would permit me to go away with my family in the school holidays, because others had booked the dates. Only one Inspector could be off at a time. I was grateful when one of my colleagues moved a week to make the holiday possible. Chief Inspector Roger Williams stated it wouldn't happen the following year, and even issued an order of priority, which as I had clearly been at the bottom would put me at the top the following year. Imagine my surprise, a year later when a colleague jumped in first. I dug my heels in. At that time there was a pop group or was it a tune called 'Frankie Goes to Hollywood', and wherever you went traffic men were to be heard saying "Frankie goes to Yugoslavia, perhaps". I had my holiday. I enjoyed it too.

We had some difficulty with the Range Rovers being used on the motorways, and one vehicle that had broken down was left overnight at the roadside. As a result when the workshops went to collect it the next morning it had been wrecked. This didn't happen when I was on duty. The next time it happened the vehicle was at Magor, and not being prepared to have a vehicle damaged I insisted that a Traffic crew turn up with a Landrover and trailer to convey it back to Headquarters. The problem was the combination of drawing vehicle and trailer was not right for such a heavy vehicle as a Range Rover. Consequently the driver Dai Morgan was lucky to get it back without mishap. The outfit had veered from side to side. I vowed this was never going to happen again. Some months later I went on duty to be told that another Range Rover had died and again it was at Magor. The instruction was clear – it was to be left at Magor overnight. I would have none of it. The vehicle was coming back that night, and not on our equipment. I rang Walls the Recovery People and was quoted what I knew was a fair price. I told them to get it back and send the bill in. After all I was paid to make decisions, wasn't I? I left the garage's advice note on the desk with a short note. and that was the end of that – or so I thought.

Next time I went on duty I was informed that I would have to account for my actions. How dare I call out Walls to recover the Range Rover. It should have stayed where it was. I duly completed my report, and left it on the desk for the morrow, realising that it was the first step on my road to the Olympics – for I was for the High Jump, no mistakes, and I'd been told so. But on the morrow fate took a hand. The Landrover and trailer had been sent to Castleton to recover a broken down Ford Granada estate. In itself not a great problem – but these vehicles carried a great deal of equipment and that bumped up the weight considerably. Imagine everyones surprise when the trailer gave up the ghost and the Granada landed on the deck at Coedkernew, and right outside Walls Garages door. I never heard anything more about my report, and no, I didn't go to the Olympics.

I realised that an officer on another shift had a problem, it was the talk of the department, but I knew nothing of the details. One evening, when my shift overlapped his he asked if he could speak to me. At that time I had been on the Police Federation for a few years, and he wanted to know how to get legal representation. He mentioned details of the case. He said that it had been alleged that he had assaulted someone on his way home from work. At the time he was supposed to have been on his push bike, but stated that he had used his car that day. He discussed details of the allegation and wondered how the Police Federation could help him. I made a few telephone calls and told him who to contact. I asked him what day did the allegation concern. He told me, and I looked in my duty diary. I could see that it was a day that I had worked nights. In fact I had worked nights on two consecutive days. I remember on the first day that there had been some kind of function in the Police Club, and that the top car park had been full, apart from one space next to his white Rover saloon. I saw that I was a witness – and immediately told him that in no circumstances would I discuss the matter further – I did not want there to be any question of my discussing the case further so as to ensure that my evidence remained untainted. He understood and left immediately.

Apparently the case revolved around an incident on what would or could have been his route home from work on the Saturday. A pedal cyclist in a blue shirt had allegedly assaulted a young man and it appeared that checks had been made to find out who it might have been. This officer had fitted the bill. The time, the route, the description, apparently all fitted. But what of the pedal cycle? I know I parked my car next to his, as being a motor cyclist for so many years, I was more used to riding straight in, and my ability, yes strange to admit but true, in reversing was not as good as it should have been. As a result when reversing in on that evening I had stopped and got out of my car to look what clearance I had. There would have been trouble if I had bumped his car. I attended at the Complaints Department and duly made a statement to the Investigating Officer.

Apparently as a result of my statement the prosecution asserted that he had driven his car home, and then gone out on his pedal cycle taking the same route. A bit weak I thought. But I attended at the Cardiff Crown Court but was not required to give evidence of his car on the night. I was present for the final addresses by council for the prosecution and defence, and the Judges summing up. I was horrified to learn that the complainant had made four statements and that the colour of the bike had changed too. He was picked out at an identification parade though, and whilst he was being interviewed on one occasion his wife had been visited at home and interviewed too without him being told. This man had been suspended from duty for almost a year before the case had come to trial. That is not quite correct. As there were two or really three trials. At the first the jury failed to agree a verdict. At the second the jury came to the same conclusion, but the Judge put a stop to it, and held the third trial then and there and acquitted him. I had given evidence of character, and when the jury in the second trial had come back for directions from the judge, they were arguing before the door had closed behind them. I told the officer that I thought he would have a hung jury a second time. He was gutted. But, I told him this judge won't allow this to go on again – and neither did he.

This officer had gone through a lot. Suffered, and his family too. For what – it wasn't exactly life threatening. But that's not the point is it? I don't believe the case against him was strong enough to merit a prosecution. From what I heard there was no question but that he was innocent. I did not like it, not one bit.

Having been acquitted by the Court, he was re-instated and promptly despatched for pastures new – to a valley town where he still serves. I imagine that his innocence has to date cost him in the region of £5,000 in petrol alone and about 4,000 hours in travelling.

Don't anyone say that Police Officers look after their own. This case dramatically disproves that particular lie.

The organisations set up for the families of victims involved in fatal road accidents, had been making their views plain for some time on the manner in which these accidents were investigated. If someone is murdered, a whole team led by an officer of some seniority is deployed to carry out the investigation. Whereas, if someone dies in a road accident, even where the other driver was responsible – through recklessness, speed or alcohol, often a single constable might be given the job of investigating the circumstances. There was some merit in their case. Not that we didn't have first rate officers capable of doing a first class job, quite the contrary. But when a man was struck off to deal, after a day or two his supervisors would be chasing to find when he would wrap it up and be back on shift proper.

Mr. Frost, the Deputy Chief Constable had discussed this with Mr. Coburn – a first class investigator, and they subscribed to the notion that a higher ranking officer should carry out the investigation. I was asked what I thought – and I couldn't argue with the reasoning. It made sound sense. Thus it was decided, for an experimental period initially, that I would actually deal with every fatal road accident which occurred when my shift was on duty. As the person in charge of the shift, I at least could make sure that I got the time to complete the investigation without bowing to pressure. And so it was.

To go into great detail would be to risk upsetting and offending those who have survived such incidents, and those left behind when a loved one has so tragically passed away. I do not wish to rake up memories for those who have so bravely managed to try and put their lives back together. As a result I will make no mention of the accidents. If accident actually explains adequately the incident when someone is killed – I think not. In the sixties and seventies about 60 to 70 people were killed on the roads in Gwent. In the eighties this had fallen to between 30 and 40, and although however tragic each case is – it was an improvement. One year the figure actually fell to 14 fatalities – the lowest since the Second World War. The reason – no, not better driving – the reason was seat belts and the breathalyser. It was the norm when arriving at a fatal road accident to find the occupants of the car thrown out onto the road suffering a further and more personal impact. But after the introduction of seat belts this went down and casualties were at least to have the benefit of the vehicle to take the impact. Alcohol. Yes people have been more sensible. and yes the younger generation have grown up with the breathalyser and have in the main got a far more sensible view than the generation that went before. Hard to believe. It shouldn't be, the Police know it's true.

The Police, of which you must have gathered I am no longer one, having retired, have done stirling work in the form of campaigns and the method of detection and patrols has improved immeasurably. But it's you the public who hold the key. It's the public – the men and women on the street who have and are changing things for the better. Your attitude has changed – and with it the behaviour which causes such tragedies has improved.

When I left the motor patrol in 1989, I was glad. How could I endure any longer the ordeal of telling loved ones that their father, mother, brother, sister, son or daughter was not coming home. If you think a Police Officer can switch off – think again. I used to go into mourning with the families, and yes on many occasions cried with them. The worst thing that can happen to anyone is to actually outlive their own children – they never recover. The pain lives with them for ever. How could it be any different?

At one accident, we the Police, Ambulance, Fire Service, Doctors and Nurses, spent hours saving a young man's life. He was permanently marked – but he lived, and was acquitted of the charge of causing death by reckless driving. I will always remember when his family walked by me outside the Crown Court absolutely jubilant, and ignored me and my colleagues – part of the very team which enabled him to be there. It hurt. It hurt us all. Another young chap, also permanently scarred with a limp for life had to continue his treatment even from Prison, but he did show remorse for his actions.

I had never dealt with the new system of interviewing, and when I interviewed a driver at Newport Central Police Station represented by Emma James the solicitor, I did not need to use notes, so vivid were the contents of the witness statements in my mind. He was honest in his interview and showed genuine remorse. I don't know how he has turned out, for I haven't heard of or seen him since the day he was sent down. But on the day I interviewed you, YOU WERE A MAN MY SON.

After about a month Mr. Frost and Superintendent Coburn decided to extend the system, and thereafter all fatal road accidents were dealt with by Traffic Inspectors.

Strange to think, having dealt with such accidents for a period of years, that a Temporary Chief Inspector when writing out my staff appraisal commented that I was far too thorough in the way I dealt with fatal road accidents. Imagine. I wasn't having that, and when I was interviewed further up the tree, said so. It was amazing – having been in the winning team, someone actually wanted me to kick the ball in the back of my own net. Can you be too thorough in dealing with the death of a fellow human being. I think not. And happily so did the Chief Constable, Mr. Over who on January 16, 1989 commended me thus:–

I COMMEND INSPECTOR PAUL HEATON FOR SUSTAINED AND CONSISTENTLY SEARCHING ENQUIRIES INTO FATAL ROAD ACCIDENTS.

The Author with Commendation Certificate at Police Headquarters on January 16, 1989. *(Gwent Constabulary)*

A Federation Representative

The Police Federation of England and Wales had been formed by Act of Parliament in 1919. It was the result of the Government Enquiry which had followed two Police strikes. Prior to 1919 there had been no national rates of pay and conditions of service within the Police Service. Such conditions and pay were initiated in that year, but at the same time officers were no longer to have the right to strike. The result was the forming of the Police Federation, and assistance with meetings and expenses. At that time the Federation could not collect subscriptions, and that was not allowed until the 1950s. Over the years its influence has grown in line with the increased services offered to its members. The Federation consists of local Branch Boards, in individual ranks – Constable, Sergeant, and Inspectors/Chief Inspectors consisting of elected members, and a Joint Branch Board where the three ranks meet together. Regionally, representatives are elected to represent the eight regions of the country, nationally on the Joint Central Committee.

The Traffic Department Inspector's representative had resigned late in 1983, and no one wanted to take on the role. As a result of discussions with Ted Simmonds the Joint Branch Board Secretary, and Mr. Edgar Shepherd, who was now employed in a civilian capacity, but had been the previous Federation Secretary, I agreed to take over the role. Thus in 1983 I embarked on my career as a Federation man. Surprisingly I had twenty years service, but I was prepared to do the job, and whilst some constables had up to a hundred members in their electorate, I had only twelve.

I attended the quarterly meetings of the Inspectors' and Joint Branch Boards, and eventually set out for the Federations Annual Conference at Scarborough in May, 1984. I sat as an observer in the Gallery and didn't miss a speech. I was disappointed that although there were issues being debated which could have an impact on our members – no one from Gwent got up and made an input. On the coach home to Gwent I made my feelings known.

The next year I went as a delegate, and made my first speech, of course it had to be on honoraria. On reflection I realise now how small minded I had been. Surely there were far more urgent issues affecting the Police Service, than how much or how little should be paid to our national officers. I remember that I waited for my turn to speak, and being an amendment to a motion was to be followed at some stage by another from Gwent who was to second me. I walked up to the rostrum and kept to my notes. As I went on my confidence rose, and eventually I plucked up enough courage to look over the notes at the audience, but was soon back with my head in my notes. The night before, Gerald Jones the Secretary from Dyfed Powys had run through my speech with me, and gave me much encouragement. Eventually I finished – yes my first speech was done, and there were more to follow, I soon overcame any nervousness. However, Roger Strong, who seconded me, and had been most confident, hadn't taken the same precaution as regards notes, and as he said later – " I nearly lost it there".

Thereafter they couldn't keep me down. I became for five years the main speaker from Gwent, and yes we always had something important to say. I enjoyed it all, every minute of it. I also enjoyed the shows put on for us by the local Mayor and the Federation on the Tuesday and Wednesday evenings of conference.

That year, 1985 was the year that Ted Simmonds came off the Joint Central Committee, and thereafter looked after just Gwent. I say just, but there was much to do. When he retired he was replaced by John Parsons a former Newport Borough man. Whereas Ted had been a county man. I had known Ted Simmonds for years, and had always had a lot of time for him. John took time to take over the reins of the office, as anyone would, but he soon got the hang of it.

It was in Blackpool in 1985 that Roy Williams decided to stand for election as Chairman of the Gwent Joint Branch Board. Paul Murphy who had recently been promoted Chief Inspector had resigned, the same having happened to his predecessor Roger Williams. It was obvious that we the board needed someone in the 'Chair' who wasn't going to disappear through a decision taken elsewhere than by the board. Roy would fit that criteria as he was a constable, never wanting to be qualified for promotion. That didn't stop me from throwing my hat into the contest. It is good for democracy for a contest to take place. It would keep whoever got the post on his toes. Anyway Roy was elected chairman, and in the event I became Vice-chairman of the board.

The year 1985 was to see changes in our Regional representation too. Whilst Quentin Lewis remained to look after the constables, Jeff Moseley had replaced Ted Simmonds, and Terry Grinter had taken over from Bill Williams from North Wales who was retiring. All three were from South Wales. Regarding Terry's position there had been much discussion the night before concerning the election, and there was some question that if we voted for a North Wales candidate, Ted would have survived in the sergeants. Each rank position belongs to their own rank – it isn't a position for deals. That was why Gwent Inspectors voted for Terry Grinter – they kept faith with a decision taken at Region. If they hadn't, Terry would never have got on. The voting at that time was a possible: South Wales – 7, North Wales – 4, Dyfed Powys – 3, Gwent – 3. South Wales could win anything if they took one other force, and could lose everything if the other three stood together. These were figures which were to stay in my mind for many years.

Conference at Scarborough in 1986 saw me limping to the platform to speak. The Saturday before I had a 'big toe nail' removed in hospital, but there was no way I was going to miss conference, and there I was in Scarborough commuting between the hotel and conference centre in the rain with what John Parsons had called my 'Jesus sandals'. Yes I had wet feet, and virtually every evening had to report to Filey Hospital to have the dressings changed. When going to the platform, I was always heavily supported by Margaret Morgan, an Inspector from Gwent. I had known Margaret way back in the 1960s when she had been a probationer at Ebbw Vale, and again at Newport where she was the sergeant in charge of the Policewomens' Section. When I needed a seconder, she was there. On one occasion standing to speak with only minutes notice, she had been magnificent.

109

Members of the Police Federation lobbying Members of Parliament over pay problems on December 16, 1976. Sergeant Ted Simmonds facing camera.

(Daily Mail)

When I had spoken for the Joint Branch Board, Roy Williams and John Parsons had always wanted to know what I was going to say – and sometimes, if the*y* were lucky I told them. On other occasions, I preferred to rise to speak on my own behalf, and often did. That was the way of it at Blackpool in 1987.

Terry Grinter, who I have always liked, and always supported, told me that he wondered if he was going to be returned as the Regional Member one year. I told himnot to worry, as Gwent, who had supported him in the beginning, would not pull the rug from under him now. We had helped put him there, and we were going to make damn sure he stayed there. He was pleased. South Wales were pleased – so much so that, having the three reserve places, they made way for me to become the First Reserve. I was pleased, and my colleagues in Gwent were pleased, too. The only problem was in May, 1988 I had two Crown Court trials running together on cases of 'Death by Reckless Driving', one in Newport, and one in Cardiff. That was the year that I had to take my place on the floor of conference to qualify to become a reserve. I did make it to Scarborough, arriving at lunch time on the Wednesday. Rushing to the hotel, I found that I was allocated to share a room with Barney, and taking my gear to the room, was surprised to see him still in bed, I think he had picked up a stomach bug or something. I was soon on the floor of conference, but that year I did not speak.

Back in Gwent I attended the meetings with the Chief Constable, Association of Chief Police Officers, the Superintendents Association with the Police Federation Joint Branch Board. These meetings were called the Joint Negotiating Consultative Committee, and were a forum suggested by Lord Edmund Davies in his report, to discuss matters of common interest regarding the welfare and efficiency of the force. I learnt some useful lessons. Never sit opposite the Chief – Mr. Over or his Deputy, Mr. Rostron, as when they spoke they always addressed you, or appeared to be. That was alright if it was a rather innocuous subject. But if it was a subject which caused heated discussion, I found that the heat was directed in my direction. Yes, far better let someone else take it. In the end we always arrived in the Conference Room early, specially reserving these warm seats for the Superintendents' Association members. A much better job. I am not prone to giving advice – but if you can possibly avoid it don't arrange a meeting on a Monday. A.C.P.O. members are different creatures at the beginning of the week – aren't we all? Far better arrange things for the Friday when all are enjoying the anticipation of the weekends pursuits. If you only stand a meagre chance of getting your own way on a Friday, you will stand absolutely no chance on a Monday. Try it and see.

When I went on the Joint Branch Board in 1983 we were ill equipped for the job. We went before the Chief Constable with matters and grievances which were poorly researched, and no account had been taken in the preparation and presentation of our case. As a result we left meetings looking and feeling like Lord Wellington's survivors. He massacred us. The result of these painful lessons, was that we quickly got our act together, became far more professional, and learnt that there were more ways of skinning a cat. Even Mr. Over recognised that we had come of age.

Gwent Constabulary Joint Branch Board – January, 1986.

Back row (left): Les Punt, Chris Morgan, Stuart Connick, Peter Fou'weather, Eric Curtis, Mike Breakwell, Dave Beacham, Alan Wright, Bill Davies (Treasurer), Ken Le Provost, Adrian Tew, S. Spiteri.
Front row: Ian Barnard, Ken Morris, Howard Salmon, Roy Williams (Chairman), John Parsons (Secretary), Sue Tuffnell, Paul Heaton.

The New Jerusalem –
Surbiton at Last

Monday, December 5, 1988 appeared like any other day. It was mild for a December day, and it was dry. My bride of six months, Veronica, was in work, and having set up home in Abergavenny town, I decided to walk the quarter mile or so to the Hen & Chicks in Flannel Street. Soon comfortably seated facing towards the door, I enjoyed my pint of Bass and two full rounds of their wonderful beef sandwiches. Only one other public house had ever served me a pint as good as this, but not better. Yes I will have a second, and indeed another round of sandwiches. It had been almost twenty five years since I had first arrived in this lovely little market town, then I had been lucky to make ten stone. But now with an appetite which could cope with three shredded wheat, I had risen in weight to a round fourteen stone. Yes I will have another pint, I'm walking – I left the car at home, and Veronica won't be home 'till eight tonight. This Bass is good – life is idyllic.

Come closing time, I made my way home – not quite as briskly as the outward journey, but I arrived at the door nonetheless. A nice cup of coffee and an afternoon snooze – yes it had been an enjoyable day off. As I put the key in the lock, I heard the telephone, we'd had trouble with it earlier and wondered if it was working properly now. I entered and picked it up. The phone crackled – Ron, Ron who? I excused myself and hurriedly ran into the kitchen splashing my face with water; that was better. Was it the man from Littlewoods? Was it the man from Vernons? No it was even better it was the man from the JCC. Yes, it was Ron Ellis – the Secretary of the Inspectors Central Committee of the Police Federation of England and Wales, ringing me from Wakefield. Ron Ellis, I knew him, but I'd never been able to get near enough to have a proper conversation. But here I was, and he was talking to me, a mere country boy from Gwent – what did he want? My head was really clear now, and I was all ears.

He told me that Terry Grinter was retiring at the end of the month, and that being the First Reserve for the Wales Region on the Joint Central Committee, was I prepared to accept the position? Was I? Just try and stop me. To be one of the members of this important committee was a great honour, after all there were only ten from each rank in the whole of England and Wales. True most did not understand what it entailed, and true I was one of them. But I had a capacity to learn, and learn I would.

Dating from 1919 the terms of reference of the Police Federation was to have an input into those matters which had a bearing on the welfare and efficiency of the Police Service. And whilst many services had been added, such as legal representation and member services, the original principles still held good. The important thing for any Representative at whatever level in the organisation was to do ones best for the membership. This was to entail representing the views of members, and in my case that was the Inspectors

Gwent Constabulary Joint Branch Board – January, 1987.

Back row (left): Ian Pritchard, Ian Barnard, Eric Curtis, Alan Wright, Albie Proctor, Mike Breakwell, P. Cole, John Evans, Ken King. *Front row*: Chris Morgan, Ken Morris, Howard Salmon, Roy Williams (Chairman), John Parsons (Secretary), Sue Tuffnell (Treasurer), Paul Heaton, John Moore.

and Chief Inspectors of Wales. Yes, the whole of Wales – North Wales, Dyfed Powys, South Wales and Gwent officers. Their interests were paramount. At the same time I still had a local electorate of twelve in Gwent, and was still Vice Chairman of the Joint Branch Board, and was now also the Secretary of the Inspector Branch Board.

On hearing that I was to become a member of the Joint Central Committee from January 1, 1989, I rang Sergeant John Parsons at Headquarters who quickly arranged for me to see the Deputy Chief Constable, Mr. Frost. I was still a Traffic Inspector in Gwent and it was important that my new role should not interfere with the operational efficiency of the force. It was arranged that whilst I should stay within the Traffic Department fold I was to undertake a Police National Computer Audit and would spend a period within the Organisation and Planning Department. Simply put, the P.N.C. is a computer which contains, nationally details of people wanted and vehicles stolen and other things of interest. The importance of auditing a computer is to ensure that nothing is on it which shouldn't be, so if a man wanted for an offence had been arrested the entry should be removed. Similarly if a car had been stolen, following its recovery it too should come off the computer. To leave them on would risk a man being arrested a second time, or an innocent owner of a vehicle being stopped or even arrested. If the normal procedures had been carried out this would be impossible. But in a world where there is such a thing as human fallibility, sometimes, fortunately rarely, the entry might not have been removed. It was my job, together with a constable allocated to assist, to ensure that this had not happened, and if we found it had, to put the error right then and there, immediately. I was to carry out these duties when not actually undertaking Federation work. The Gwent Constabulary were most supportive of me. Mr. Over liked men from Gwent holding National positions, and thought quite rightly that it was good for the force, it put Gwent on the map – where I must say it always was, as we were an above average force for one so small. Everyone had heard of Gwent. Mr. Over ensured that I was given every facility – I was grateful.

I had never visited the offices of the Police Federation at 15, 17 and 19, Langley Road, Surbiton, Surrey, as a result, Quentin Lewis, the Constables' Regional Representative from South Wales kindly offered to take me when he had to visit on January 4 for a Discipline Sub-Committee meeting. I met him at Newport Central Police Station, and went up as a passenger in his car. Stopping at Fred's Diner at Sunbury I met Garry Hyde, a fellow Inspector's rep from the West Midlands who was also on his way to the meeting. Breakfast complete, we continued the journey, arriving at the offices at about eight in the morning. As anyone who knows Quentin will vouch, I couldn't have had a better companion that day to show me around the Headquarters of the Federation. Quentin knows everyone, and everyone knows Quentin. He introduced me to every person in the building – and there were rather a lot, and showed me every office, nook and cranny. Apart from being a member of the JCC Quentin was the Joint Branch Board Secretary in South Wales, operating from offices in Briton Ferry. He was popular, but like myself a

Joint Central Committee of the Police Federation of England and Wales at a Statutory Meeting at Bournemouth in March, 1989.
Back row (left): Mick Gray, Billy Braben, Ron Ellis, Garry Hyde, Brian Turrell, Quentin Lewis, Alan Turner, Jeff Moseley, Steve Barrett, *Middle row*: Paul Middup, Charlie McIlwrick, Ernie Gash, Paul Heaton, Len Cantliffe, Brian Payne, Barrie Biddulph, Dennis Forsyth, Stuart Cadmore, Maureen Henderson, Paul Rabbeth, Helen Lewis, Paul O'Brien, Norman Mackett, Peter Cripps. *Front row*: John Thompson (Deputy Treasurer), Trevor Laws (Treasurer), Vi Nield (General Secretary), Alan Eastwood (Chairman), Dick Coyles (Vice Chairman), Lyn Williams (Deputy Secretary). (Police Federation of England and Wales)

Police Federation Annual Conference at Blackpool in 1989.

(*Reproduced by Kind Permission of Lewis Productions Ltd.*)

trifle overweight, and yes by now my hair had, like his, disappeared.

I met the Chairman of the Federation, Alan Eastwood, yes the man himself. He put me at ease and was most amiable, the warmth of his welcome quite stunned me. I was invited to sit through the Discipline Sub-Committee as an observer, and I met other members of the Committee. Alan sat as Chairman of this sub-committee, he always believing, quite rightly that it was one of the most important. The Secretary of Discipline was John 'Geordie' Thompson from Gloucester. What this man didn't know about discipline wasn't worth knowing. He and Peter Cripps were the two acknowledged experts in this field.

The problem when you are meeting people for the first time, and particularly when there were so many new faces to see, is that you don't absorb too much – and it's only after a few meetings that they actually register in your mind. That was such a day, but I did get to know them – oh yes.

The following week I attended at Surbiton for the Statutory Meeting. Statutory, because there are six held each year and have been since the formation of the organisation and were defined by Parliament. The thirty members converged on Surrey, usually on the Monday from all parts of the country, from Cumbria and Durham in the north, Glamorgan in the west and Norfolk in the east. Yes Surbiton is in the south. Although there are eight regions in the country, there are ten members from each rank, that is because Nos. 1 – 7 Regions have one per rank, whilst the No. 8 Region representing the Metropolitan and City of London Police has two. The tenth members are the ladies, there being a female representing women specifically in each rank nationally. Happily billeted in the Richmond Hill Hotel, I found that the majority of the Inspectors stayed there. Whilst next door the Richmond Gate Hotel was home for the week for many others. Whilst Surbiton has a substantial full time staff, and they are needed – the main figures in the organisation have offices there, full time officers such as chairman, vice-chairman, secretary, deputy secretary, treasurer and deputy treasurer of Joint, whilst the secretary of constables and sergeants actually have offices in no. 19 Langley Road. The Inspectors was an itinerant post – their secretary having offices where ever the holder happened to be stationed, thus Ron Ellis being a West Yorkshire man operated from Wakefield – but this changed.

On that first night I was introduced to the Green Bottle Club. Green, because it contained gin, not my drink – I preferred whisky, happily one or two others did. This club was something of an institution, those who stayed at the Richmond Hill, or those who wanted met in one or others room, daily following the business of the day and having driven back from Surbiton. It was mostly made up of Inspectors, Brian Turrell the Inspectors' chairman, Ron Ellis the secretary, Alan Turner the vice-chairman, Garry Hyde deputy secretary, Norman Mackett from Hampshire. Paul Rabbeth the Federation Training Coordinator was an infrequent visitor, as was Len Cantliffe who stayed next door. Vi Nield the JCC General Secretary stayed elsewhere, whilst Charlie McIlwrick commuted from home daily. The other, the only other permanent member of the Green Bottle Club was 'Geordie' Thompson, deputy treasurer of joint and a sergeant.

Brian Turrell a man from Leicestershire was approaching or had just reached his fifties, he was a fairly blunt individual and was proud that he had been a miner. Ron Ellis was an astute person who had been a Traffic Man in Yorkshire, and his youthful appearance belied his true age. Alan Turner who was the secretary of the Metropolitan Inspectors was due to retire later in the year on age limit. Garry Hyde was a proactive Midlander who was able to keep his finger on the button, he always knew what was going on, and appeared to have Alan Eastwood's ear. If you wanted something – Garry was your man, he could fix anything. Norman Mackett was the only Chief Inspector on the committee and he departed after a couple of years to resume his career in force. John Thompson was a shrewd very knowledgeable chap who had an encyclopaedia of jokes and funny stories. In Gloucester he was the Federation chairman, and if you wanted to go anywhere in the committee he was a man you had to know.

Vi Nield had been the first female holder of the post of secretary in the history of the organisation, and if there ever should be another, she would be a hard act to follow. She threw herself into her work – she believed in the 'hands on' approach, and whilst I didn't always agree with her, you just had to admire her dedication – did she ever go home? Charlie McIlwrick, I hope I've spelt it right, was a Metropolitan man, chairman of their Inspectors. He originated in Ireland and his father had been a London Bobby before him, a long time before him. Charlie was to celebrate a century of family association with the Met, as his father had joined in the 1890s and on retiring returned to Ireland where his son had arrived when he was in his seventies. Complicated – again I hope I've got it right. Len Cantliffe was from Merseyside, but had served earlier in Cheshire, almost in Wales – he was a man of few words, but those he spoke were usually worth listening too. Then there was Paul Rabbeth from Avon and Somerset, a true ideas man, the danger for Paul was there was little room for anyone with ideas on the committee. He had joined Bristol City Police originally and had been selected for the Special Course at Bramshill, where accelerated promotion was almost assured. Having obtained his LIB (Bachelor of Law) he had become involved with the Federation, if he hadn't he would without any doubt have reached some high office in the service. He had talent, but at Surbiton he had the post of Training Coordinator, arranging all Federation Training and courses. Talent such as his should have been harnessed to the benefit of the organisation. He had a lot to offer, an awful lot. Yes, it's clear from what I have said, he was a friend, a true friend of mine, one of the few I had on the Inspector's Committee.

I always preferred the company of constables, even sinfully voting with them on one or two occasions against my own. Yes how dare I! The thing is, if a man is right, it doesn't matter what rank he is. If you feel your own are wrong, be damned and vote for 'right'. The chairman of the constables was Steve Barrett, a man I kept at arms length for quite a while. But gradually as I got to know him, grew to like him, and regarded him with the respect that a true professional deserved. Steve gave wise council to the committee on many occasions. On the Thursday lunchtime of the 1990 conference at Scarborough he was sitting alone eating his sandwiches. I joined him, and he spoke a lot of sense. I commented about the ship anchored off the town – "I wonder how many foreign delegates came on her". He was very bright, very very bright – and many of you will remember his farewell speech later that afternoon – he didn't miss it, no not he. Alas he was only to enjoy a year in retirement before he was suddenly called away. But we remember you. Oh yes.

The Constables secretary was Peter Cripps, a Norfolk man I recall. An expert on discipline, there were many who had cause to thank him. He would cut his hand off to see that justice prevailed. But he did have a nasty little habit of trying to put me down in committee, and it took courage, yes mine, to stand up to his tongue. Lyn Williams a Met. man was the Deputy Secretary of Joint, and I think vice-chairman of constables. He was the man who organised so effectively the representation of members. He has a keen mind and stores a wealth of knowledge and experience. Yes, he is a Welshman – could he be anything else? Stuart Cadmore was deputy secretary of constables. A pleasant chap from Plymouth. When he was putting a point I always enjoyed seeing the twinkle in his eyes, particularly if he was swimming alone. He once challenged some minutes, and I alone voted with him – because he was right. When I did the same some months later I stood alone, he thinking I was wrong. But I was right. In fact when I spoke I often used the phrase "Am I right or am I right" – could I ever be wrong.

There was Trevor Laws from Staffordshire, who as the Joint Treasurer, had steered the organisation's finances like a true statesman. Mick Gray from Hampshire who was their Chairman and always had a sensible view. Billy Braben who was to become chairman of constables, he was a kindly figure from Merseyside. Yes kindly, a word I have not used before. The ladies in the constables were represented by Maureen Henderson from Durham. A no nonsense woman, she had a knack of always being first with the news – she certainly knew what was going on before me, and when she spoke I sat up in my seat, not wanting to miss a word. Well done Maureen. Then there was Paul Middup, the secretary of South Yorkshire, and a JCC member for, was it a decade or more? He could be sharp, and you rarely messed with him. Although I found him fair, and he certainly put the views of his region with vigour.

Then we get to the sergeants. Alan Eastwood himself. I suppose I thought him arrogant, but no I think he was just very forceful. His crime, if it be a crime, was to want to propel the organisation forward at a speed and a pace which it didn't appear ready for. They hadn't reckoned on Alan Eastwood though and for the five years that he was Chairman he dragged the Federation, often kicking and certainly screaming, towards the next Century. He certainly must take the credit for improving our image, and the professionalism that has been our hallmark was achieved during his period of leadership. He often got into trouble with others of the committee, and there were some heated debates, but come the arrival of the train it was usually Alan who was the driver and it travelled on the line that he had selected. The train never went slowly.

Dick Coyles, his deputy was a different story, I had thought at one time that he was the natural successor for the chair – even before Alan retired. He was that man who had on occasions to sort out a problem, in many ways more outspoken than Alan, he made no bones about his politics. He too had a useful input, but he never managed to acquire the flair for upsetting people that Alan had. Jeff Moseley my Regional colleague was an all questioning man. When the Legislation sub-committee minutes were dealt with at Joint he often gave me some anxious moments with his questions, and I did extra research to ensure I didn't get caught napping. He was a sergeant's man, and did everything in his power to promote the ranks influence. He upset people, but I liked him. Denis Forsyth a Warwickshire based Scot, a non-smoking connoisseur of whisky was deputy chairman of the rank. I once turned up at a statutory meeting with a bottle of Welsh whisky – that showed him. Helen Lewis from Durham was our expert on Children and Young Persons, always dealing with that aspect in Legislation. Ernie Gash from Humberside was a jovial sort and whilst I remember him for some of his good work, he will never be forgotten for his bright 'shocking' ties. Barrie Biddulph, a Met man was one of the more youthful members who was renowned for his sense of humour. Paul O'Brien was an expert on pensions and nearly became a specialist in airships, whilst Brian Payne from Derbyshire soon departed on promotion. Brian had once served in Gwent, I remembered him well.

The first working day of a Statutory Meeting is reserved for an all day meeting of the separate ranks. The constables and sergeants having their own conference rooms, we the semi-homeless Inspectors used the Goodsall Room, the JCC conference room, where the joint meeting was held on the Wednesday and Thursday, and sometimes even the Friday.

Of the six statutory meetings, four were held at Surbiton, and two out in the country. At the outside meetings an open meeting was held to update the membership. Eventually the six meetings were centred on Surbiton and when an open meeting was needed that was arranged when there was actually something to say. Better to have an open meeting when the need was clear, than have officers travelling all over the country to attend a meaningless meeting, where the message was just a repeat of what they already knew. Keep it relevant, much better.

On my first meeting I was appointed to the Discipline Sub-Committee, a very busy and important group, which met regularly, and the Leave Sub-Committee, which could go for months without a meeting. I was lucky that Brian Turrell had intervened as otherwise goodness knows what I would have been allocated. After a couple of years I took up a position on Legislation which was a very busy committee, one which I particularly enjoyed.

It took about a year to get to know where I was going. Yes a whole year. It takes time to acclimatise to the work, and know the background of subjects. Yes this was no job for anyone making just a quick visit. Continuity was the name of the game.

Foreign Climes

Part of my duty related to updating Inspectors Branch Boards within my region on developments in Federation matters and involved making periodic visits to North Wales at Colwyn Bay, Dyfed Powys at Carmarthen, South Wales at Bridgend as well as my own in Gwent. On occasions I was asked to update the whole Joint Branch Board. I usually went to Colwyn Bay and Carmarthen twice yearly, but South Wales wanted me for all four of their meetings. I was always made most welcome. In the early days my inexperience showed, as my briefings were short, but as time went by I was able to give far better and more interesting updates. I was always supported by my region in magnificent style. Loyalty counts for a lot.

I also attended the four Regional meetings usually held at Newtown in mid-Wales. I found these meetings to be something of an ordeal, and often felt that I knew at first hand what it was like to be a coconut at the funfair. The problem was, that those attending Region only had this forum to vent their feelings, and feelings there were on occasions. Quentin, and latterly Roy Williams, and Jeff Moseley and I shared the update. Jeff who had been on the Police Negotiating Board, that body responsible for Police pay, allowances and pensions, having first hand knowledge of this usually gave this part of the briefing, and we were all supportive of each other, and the body we represented.

July 13, 1989 was an interesting day, altogether. Having dealt with a discipline in Gwent in the morning, I had to set out for London with my wife. That was the day we attended a Garden Party at Buckingham Palace. Leaving Abergavenny at 1p.m., we stopped in a hotel in the heart of the Capital to change, having reserved a room for a few hours. We emerged, I in morning suit and she in her new outfit, and just arrived a few minutes before Her Majesty and her party. What a lovely day. I had started at around seven in the morning and arrived home at past midnight, and I was back at a meeting the following day.

The Police Federation of England and Wales had been members of Union International Syndicates de Policia (U.I.S.P.) for a number of years. I was one of those nominated to attend their Congress, a three yearly event at Esjberg in Denmark. I decided to take my wife, as by now she rarely saw me, and duly coughed up the £300 plus to take her. Departing from Heathrow on a Monday morning and returning on the Friday afternoon. Our accommodation was at a training establishment for Trade Unions, and we were housed in Block K (not H). It was an interesting visit, and the congress was an opportunity to meet others from our profession in Europe. Another visit about a month later was to the statutory meeting at Belfast between England and Wales with our counterparts in Scotland and Northern Ireland. Again I took my wife, and yes, again, I paid the princely sum of £320 for flight and two nights away. We enjoyed our visit and made some lovely friends in the R.U.C. We had felt it proper for both of us to visit Ireland. We on our side of the Irish Sea have much to admire in our friends in the Royal Ulster Constabulary.

Dave Hayward, who replaced Brian Payne on the Sergeants Committee, and I once flew to Germany to attend a Media Training Course at the International Police Association's Training establishment at Schloss Gimborne, near Cologne. Whilst the accommodation was not the most palatial I had enjoyed it was adequate, and the food although totally local usually had something to tempt me. The cost of full board for one week had worked out at £50, a very reasonable figure. Really good value. The setting of the I.P.A. school was idyllic, but unfortunately it rained all the time. The idea of sending us was to evaluate all organisations involved in Europe for the Police Service. We reported our findings, even recommending that others should go the following year, as yes they ran courses in the English language. Imagine our surprise when Dave French and Tony Mason who went, escaped over the wall a day or so early. It must have been hell.

It had been decided in 1992 that Paul Rabbeth would attend the International Association of Chiefs of Police in Detroit. In the event he could not go, and yes, lucky me I was sent. Also on the plane was Denis Forsyth and Tony Mason, and Tony Judge was already out there having written articles on Policing in Canada. Yes it was Club Class, and why not? Do you honestly expect people who are continuously away from their families to slum it? The Police Federation has come to mean something, and not a penny pinching cowboy outfit. The Federation internationally is held up as one of the Jewels in the Crown. Everywhere you go – "The Federation, tell me . . .?" Yes Alan Eastwood you had done well. That could only be good for the men and women who protect us all in Britain. You have status, recognise it.

Returning to Detroit, I sat on the plane with a senior officer from the R.U.C., a most agreeable fellow, and he smoked too. Denis and Tony who didn't were at the front. Arriving at the hotel, we found it to be one of, if not the highest building in the area. We booked in, they on the 26th floor and I on the 42nd. In fact there were 89 floors. On arrival in my room, I peeped out of the window, and my how my feet sweat. My fear of heights came rushing back. It took me a full day to pluck up enough courage to reach out and close the curtains, and I even considered sleeping in the bathroom. What a hell of a way up.

On the morrow we registered at the conference centre, a truly huge affair, and later on had some free time. Denis was anxious to have a look at golf clubs, and had been told of a shop a shortish distance away. Or so we thought. We caught the bus, and about one or one and a half hours later arrived at a truly exceptional sporting equipment shop. The problem was the journey, it was memorable to say the least. Tony thought we might have been mugged. I didn't. I have seen poverty like this before – I was more concerned about T.B. We went into the shop and Denis was shown an enormous range of clubs. After about half an hour looking around, I got bored. Golf is not my game, remember. So I went outside and next door was a restaurant, as the patrons drove up to it, they got out of their cars and one of two girls in their thirties parked them. Apparently I was told they had been doing this for a decade, and made a healthy living off the tips. What a sound business idea for someone. I could have done it whilst I was waiting.

After a short walk and it was back to the Golf shop, I had been at least an hour, and Denis was still deciding on what club to buy. In the end he decided on one called 'Big Bertha', and because it had been used before there was a reduction of some kind. So my first afternoon had been spent, on a bus – two to three hours, and in or around a golf shop – another two hours at least. We did have a meal in the restaurant next door, and isn't food in America such good value?

We soon met up with Tony Judge, and he was his usual excellent company. But I have always been a loner, and thereafter there were to be no more golf shops. I rose at six each morning and after an excellent eat and drink as much as you like breakfast, I was at the conference centre for the early morning workshops and lectures. I attended them on Weed and Seed, no not gardening – the resettling of problem people, the fight against motor crime – yes in America, or at least in three states there is an extra Dollar put on insurance premiums to enable initiatives to be taken against car theft. It works too. It could come to Britain. It took two days to explore the exhibition and that was remarkable. So many guns. The business in the main hall was interesting, and Mr Bush campaigning for the White House came too, he didn't make it that year. Mr Clinton, who did, arrived the very day of our departure. Such was the status of this conference. I tended to go my own way, and in the evenings accepted invitations from the F.B.I. and someone campaigning as a Vice-President of I.A.C.P. to their suites, where I met a lot of interesting people, and enjoyed the odd drink or two. Yes they were excellent hosts, they valued your presence, and they looked after you.

I didn't see much of Denis and Tony, who attended other lectures, but I saw a lot of Chief Officers and Police Authority people from Britain, and I made contacts which were of use to our organisation. One idea which the Police Federation may like, was that when you entered the conference main hall you were given a ticket with a number on it, and every hour or two, just to make sure the venue was full, a number was drawn, prizes ranging from $200 to $500 were given. I didn't win, but a number within six of mine was drawn one day.

This was the conference that there was so much trouble over the previous year. So much so, that a Committee of Enquiry was set up. There was one from each rank on the committee. I was selected from the Inspectors' Committee. No one else seemed to be eligible, I wondered why. Jeff Vince was the sergeant and Maureen Henderson the constable. I had not been Alan Eastwood's biggest fan up till then. And I understood that Alan was not excited with two of the people allocated to do the job. He needn't have worried, it's one thing to be cleared by a friend, but it must be sheer bloody magic to be exonerated by a critic. The terms of reference were to look into the circumstances of the trip to Minneapolis to I.A.C.P. in 1991. In particular the uprating of travel returning to Britain by Club Class, and in general the level of expenses. Well there was a need to uprate – there was a flaw in the Federation's booking of travel which was soon identified. And the level of expenditure was even less than a statutory meeting. I was disturbed by the numbers of 'Don't mention my name'-people who were trying to point us in this and that direction. I couldn't believe how much bad blood there was. No Alan Eastwood, you need have had no fear, as Maureen, Jeff and I were certainly not going to fire bullets at you. Not bullets made by others. Certainly not. And that is how Alan Eastwood obtained a fan. Yes, after that I vowed to support him, as support he clearly needed. There are enough people out there trying to harm us without us harming ourselves, needlessly.

I almost forgot, I had a meal in the roof restaurant at Detroit, alone. I went up in the outside lift to the top floor, yes 89, and the lift was one of those outside ones, yes like in the film 'Towering Inferno'. Long before I reached the top I was welded against the door, petrified. I got out and was shown to a window table, it being a revolving restaurant, just in time to see a helicopter go by, well below. I soon changed seats.

Back in Surbiton, the Inspectors changed hotels going out to a place called the Monkey Puzzle. The Green Bottle Club continued, but without me. I decided that lemonade, tea and coffee were more to my liking. I was becoming a loner, a real loner.

Back in September 1990 in preparation for Trevor Law's retirement a Treasurer Elect was elected at the Carmarthen Statutory Meeting. There were two candidates, Barrie Biddulph, a sergeant, and Len Cantliffe, an inspector. I voted for Barrie as I felt that he had more years to offer the organisation, although Len was an excellent candidate. The following year the post of Deputy Treasurer became vacant on Geordie Thompson's retirement, and Len decided to stand. At the statutory meeting before the Bournemouth Conference Brian Turrell said that he hoped that we would all support Len, and there it should have ended. But no he said 'no one has been got at have they, no one has already promised their vote?' That was it. He was looking at me when he said it. No I had not promised my vote. No I had not been got at. But I stood for Deputy Treasurer myself. I was damned sure I wasn't going to be insulted.

I was surprised at the level of my support. Len had Garry Hyde as his campaign manager. I had one, but he deserted me three days before the election. I still wasn't disgraced, and you should have seen my C.V. I lost 18-12 – no I wasn't disgraced, and honour was satisfied. Show a bull a red rag and he'll attack you. Insult a Welshman and heaven knows what he'll do. So be warned!

At the Carmarthen meeting, as it was likely to be the only time the Committee was to visit Wales during my period I invited everyone, all thirty members and the staff to come and have lunch and break their journey at our home. We had an excellent day, the weather was fine, and the flowers Alan sent my wife afterwards were a much appreciated gesture.

I spent a considerable amount of my time undertaking training courses for Federation Representatives, and in all must have been Course Director on forty or more. I enjoyed this work. You got to know people who were often the Branch Board officers of tomorrow. At Conference I knew as many as anyone, and probably more. I once did a course at Hull, and the other lecturers not having turned up at the appointed time, meant I had to cover all the subjects. I tried to ring Paul Rabbeth, but was unable to contact him, so I sent a postcard – first-class, with 'help' written on it. That got a response.

Many new members arrived on the JCC during my five years. On the Inspectors' committee, there was Ray Oakley, a really smooth operator, who was the Metropolitan Inspectors' Secretary – he replaced Brian Turrell as Chairman of the Inspectors' Central Committee. Then there was the Surrey Joint Branch Board Chairman, Robin Penn, an ambitious man who is Chairman of the Legislation sub-committee. Jan Berry, in the Kent Chair replaced Vi. She has talent, so I'll be particularly interested to see how she progresses in the organisation. Then there are Brian Burdiss from Northampton and Mick Sample from Cleveland. Those last few months on the committee saw the arrival of people that I was able to start identifying with. Why couldn't they have arrived before? Oh, and I nearly forgot Brian Payne, he attended for one meeting as an Inspector.

The first new sergeant was Dave Hayward. Dave is an ideas man, with an appetite for hard work. Jeff Vince from Dorset was unusual in that he was prepared to swim against the tide – when he thought he was right he wasn't afraid to nail his colours up. I don't think Jeff was too popular, but I liked him, oh yes. Then there is Gloria Hughes from Dyfed Powys, who took over from Helen Lewis. She has become Deputy Secretary of sergeants. A knowledgeable Clint Elliott arrived from the North East, and John Harrison who I had met on a course some years ago turned up from the Met.

They tell me that Dave French has become Chairman of Constables, is he really? His mate Tony Mason has replaced Stuart Cadmore as the Constables' Secretary. I once told Tony on a Discipline Course at Torquay that he was black and white, and that he needed to find some grey. I hope he listened. Not connected with him, but interesting, on that same course I told a few of the students that I wouldn't want them representing me at my Inquest. Then there is Ken Crossman from the North East, who I never got to know. Roy Williams from Gwent, a true friend, and as sound as a pound, arrived in the middle of controversy. Brian Pallant from Essex who knows what he's about is another I particularly liked. He has the ability to put his view and at the same time recognise anothers. A rare JCC quality. Ian Westwood came from Manchester. He is ambitious and I understand that he drew the long straw, or was it heads to become Vice-Chairman of Joint. No matter, he has a wealth of knowledge and I'm sure that he will support his new Chairman. That just leaves Fred. Yes Fred Broughton, the one I always knew was the one to watch. He replaced Dick Coyles as Chairman of the Joint Central Committee of the Police Federation of England and Wales. A big imposing man who could well be a Chief Officer, let alone a Met. Constable, so well does he fit the part. My message to Fred is, I hope you get the support that you need. I know that you will put those we serve, the men and women out there in the real world, those that make England and Wales a safer place to be, first. The membership need have no fear, here is the man to lead you into the next century – here is the man you need to pledge your support to, here is the man who will see you get fair play. What I particularly like is, he's the one I would have chosen. It's nice to be on the winning side for a change. I wish you well.

In South Wales, the new Chief Constable was Bob Lawrence, who had started his Police career in West Wales. He had been an Inspector in Regional Training when I had undertaken a Newly Promoted Sergeants' Course at Croesyceiliog in the seventies. I well remember Chief Inspector Stan Raven telling the Gwent men that they should be entertaining those from other forces and not going home at night. Well we did that, and two or three weeks later the same Stan Raven scolded us for our behaviour, out every night, didn't we have homes to go to, what an example we were, he was ashamed of us. Yes Bob Lawrence was a co-conspirator on the entertainments committee.

Whilst in South Wales, Quentin Lewis departed, and was replaced by John Prosser. Their Chairman being Roy Hillman, like all the Welsh Force inspectors, a true friend and supporter. I remember at one conference at the Inspectors' bash, almost, or was it all, of the Inspectors Board, attended. In coming years they could, but only a certain number had a drink supplied.

Whilst I think of it, I had acquired a small flock of sheep, and everyone was amused by their names, as each was named after a JCC member – in line with their personalities:–

A. Kept getting caught up in barbed wire, and might finish up in the abbatoir.

B. Kept finding holes in the fence, but didn't want anyone else to find them.

C. Kept finding holes in the fence but didn't know what to do about them.

D. Didn't know which field he was in; and so on.

I mentioned earlier, continuity is the name of the game. How was it achieved? Well some will dispute what I write. But it was Tony Judge who gave us that all important continuity. Tony had joined the Police Service in 1953, and had been a member of the Joint Central Committee representing constables from 1957 to 1962. In that latter year he left the Police Service to become assistant to the Joint Central Committee Secretary, in a civilian capacity. He founded the Police Magazine for us in 1968, of which he was Editor for many years. Thereafter he was Director of Public Relations, and latterly Head of Corporate Affairs. It is all too easy to omit to mention Tony's role. Some would say that they don't like him. That may be so. But here is a man who has served under twelve different chairmen – Bert Beavitt, Syd Vass, Charles White, Derek Needham, Reg Webb, Reg Gale, Les Male, Jim Jardine, Leslie Curtis, Alan Eastwood, Dick Coyles and Fred Broughton. Yes, here was your continuity.

The Police Federation have used Russell, Jones and Walker as their solicitors for years. Some say that we should have our own in-house lawyers. They are wrong. R.J.W. have grown with us, as we have become more expert, so have they. You could not replace that experience. My advert complete – yes R.J.W. I have learnt from you – this manuscript is to be vetted by a barrister – as you surely will. No photocopying though.

Incidentally my reserve on the Inspectors' Central Committee was by now

Ray Hughes from North Wales. I could have no hesitation in commending him, as he like me had sailed in Lamport & Holt's *S.S. Romney,* as a boy. He knew Santos, too.

Tragically, John Parsons, from Gwent, died and his place as joint branch board secretary was taken by Stuart Connick. The Gwent chairman was now Howard Salmon, who in those bygone days in Abergavenny was a cadet in traffic.

Whatever the final result of the Sheehy Enquiry, the men and women of the Police Service in England and Wales, and for that matter Scotland and Northern Ireland, can be justly proud of the manner in which their elected representatives carried out the campaign. Anyone who was at Wembley would have been impressed by the professionalism of the organisation – yes we had come of age.

A number of people left the committee in 1993. Alan Eastwood left after conference, or a month or so after. It was a pity, as he had thirty years in. He was replaced by Dick Coyles in the chair – who knew what to do. Ernie Gash had thirty in and left the committee earlier to carry on his service elsewhere. It was a shame, that the sergeants didn't sort their thirty year rule out before.

Having described the arrival of a new Chairman a page or two before the departure of the old, a trait I must have picked up at Surbiton, I omitted to finish my message to Fred Broughton. Fred, when I was trained as a motor cyclist, I was always told not to take for granted what I saw in the mirror, as the view was often distorted. To get an accurate view of behind – far better to look over one's shoulder.

At the end of 1993 Gwent's Chief Constable, John Over retired, I wish him well. His replacement is Anthony Burden, who I hope will enjoy his new life in Wales. I also hope that he resists any thoughts of amalgamation; he has inherited one of the best Police Forces in the country, it will serve him well and I hope he will serve it with equal vigour. My best wishes go to him and the Gwent Constabulary.

On December 29, 1993, I decided that having completed thirty years service it was time for me to say farewell, and I formally retired from the Police Force – from the Gwent Constabulary. Farewell, my friends.

Compassion

If your son or daughter should be about to join the Police Service, impress on them the need for compassion. It has more than once been said in front of me – "Look at him", meaning a criminal or whatever. My message to those that talk like that is, we are all accidents of our own birth. I was fortunate, I was born in the right bed. There are others less fortunate who having been born in the wrong one, have never had the benefits or the privileges I have enjoyed and taken for granted. Spare a thought for those who have not had the chances in life that others have selfishly taken for granted. Whatever a person's gender, colour or station in life – we are all God's creatures – and we should remember it.

I have only one wish before I take that road skywards, that I may be permitted to take a message with me – 'There was Justice and Compassion in the Gwent Constabulary'. There is still time.

Anthony Burden – Chief Constable of Gwent from 1994.   *(South Wales Argus)*

The Author with the Leader of the Opposition – Neil Kinnock, MP, at the Headquarters of the Police Federation at Surbiton the week before the 1992 General Election.   *(John Pennington)*

The Author speaking from the Platform at the Police Federation Annual Conference.
(John Pennington)

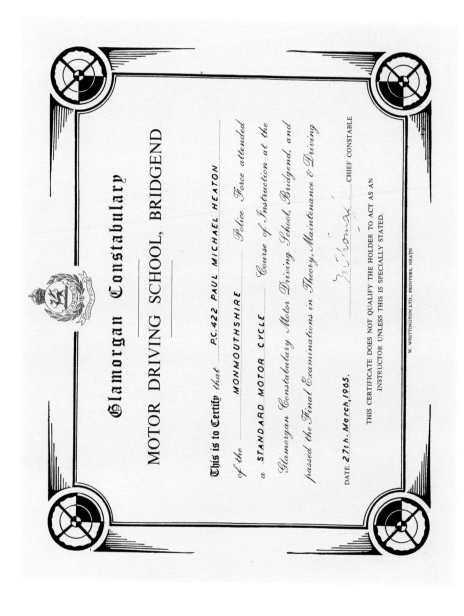

Glamorgan Constabulary

MOTOR DRIVING SCHOOL, BRIDGEND

This is to Certify that P.C.422 PAUL MICHAEL HEATON of the MONMOUTHSHIRE Police Force attended a STANDARD MOTOR CYCLE Course of Instruction at the Glamorgan Constabulary Motor Driving School, Bridgend, and passed the Final Examinations in Theory, Maintenance & Driving

DATE 27th March, 1965.

CHIEF CONSTABLE

THIS CERTIFICATE DOES NOT QUALIFY THE HOLDER TO ACT AS AN INSTRUCTOR UNLESS THIS IS SPECIALLY STATED.

W. WHITTINGTON LTD., PRINTERS, NEATH

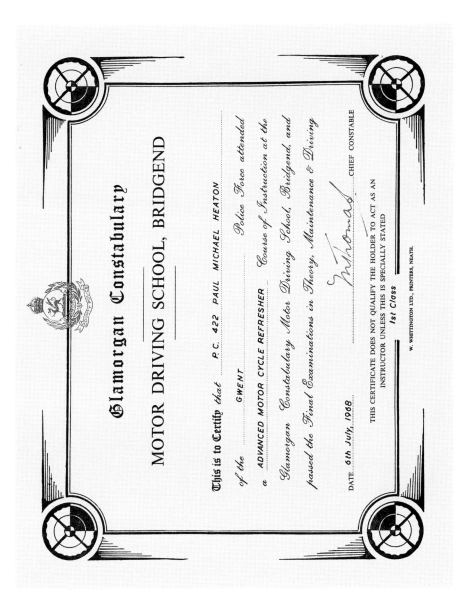

Glamorgan Constabulary

MOTOR DRIVING SCHOOL, BRIDGEND

This is to Certify that   P.C. 422 PAUL MICHAEL HEATON

of the   GWENT   Police Force attended

a   ADVANCED MOTOR CYCLE REFRESHER   Course of Instruction at the

Glamorgan Constabulary Motor Driving School, Bridgend, and

passed the Final Examinations in Theory, Maintenance & Driving

DATE   6th July, 1968

CHIEF CONSTABLE

THIS CERTIFICATE DOES NOT QUALIFY THE HOLDER TO ACT AS AN
INSTRUCTOR UNLESS THIS IS SPECIALLY STATED

1st Class

W. WHITTINGTON LTD, PRINTERS, NEATH.

133

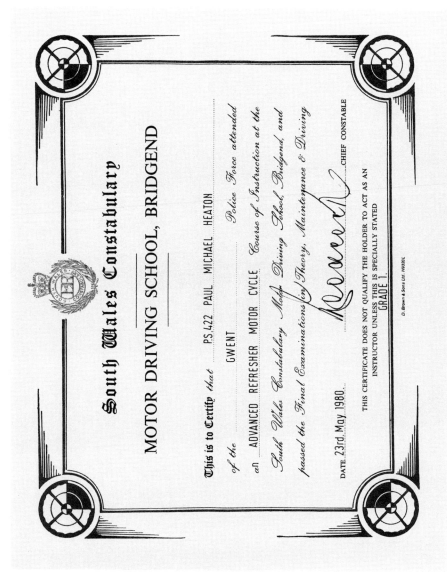

South Wales Constabulary

MOTOR DRIVING SCHOOL, BRIDGEND

This is to Certify that ...... P.S.422 PAUL MICHAEL HEATON ......

of the ...... GWENT ...... Police Force attended

an ...... ADVANCED REFRESHER MOTOR CYCLE ...... Course of Instruction at the

South Wales Constabulary Motor Driving School, Bridgend, and

passed the Final Examinations in Theory, Maintenance & Driving

DATE ...... 23rd May 1980 ......

...... CHIEF CONSTABLE

THIS CERTIFICATE DOES NOT QUALIFY THE HOLDER TO ACT AS AN
INSTRUCTOR UNLESS THIS IS SPECIALLY STATED

GRADE 1.

D. Brown & Sons Ltd. H9396L

134